THE BOOK OF

CHICKEN
DISHES

THE BOOK OF

CHICKEN DISHES

KERENZA HARRIES & JO CRAIG

Photographed by
JON STEWART

Published by Salamander Books Limited
LONDON • NEW YORK

Published 1993 by Salamander Books Limited
129-137 York Way, London N7 9LG, United Kingdom

ISBN 0-86101-747-1

Distributed by Hodder & Stoughton Services, PO Box 6,
Mill Road, Dunton Green, Sevenoaks, Kent TN13 2XX

Managing Editor: Felicity Jackson
Art Director: Roger Daniels
Editor: Louise Steele
Photographer: Jon Stewart, assisted by Nicole Mai
Home Economists: Kerenza Harries and Jo Craig
Typeset by: BMD Graphics, Hemel Hempstead
Colour separation by: Scantrans Pte. Ltd, Singapore
Printed in Belgium by Proost International Book Production

ACKNOWLEDGEMENTS

The Publishers would like to thank the following for their help and advice:
Barbara Stewart at Prop Exchange, Unit F,
51 Calthorpe Street, London WC1.

Notes:
All spoon measurements are equal.
1 teaspoon = 5 ml spoon
1 tablespoon = 15 ml spoon.

CONTENTS

COMPANION VOLUMES OF INTEREST:

The Book of SOUPS
The Book of COCKTAILS
The Book of CHOCOLATES & PETITS FOURS
The Book of HORS D'OEUVRES
The Book of GARNISHES
The Book of BREAKFASTS & BRUNCHES
The Book of PRESERVES
The Book of SAUCES
The Book of DESSERTS
The Book of ICE CREAMS & SORBETS
The Book of GIFTS FROM THE PANTRY
The Book of PASTA
The Book of HOT & SPICY NIBBLES-DIPS-DISHES
The Book of CRÊPES & OMELETTES
The Book of FONDUES
The Book of CHRISTMAS FOODS
The Book of BISCUITS
The Book of CHEESECAKES
The Book of CURRIES & INDIAN FOODS
The Book of PIZZAS & ITALIAN BREADS
The Book of SANDWICHES
The Book of SALADS
The Book of GRILLING & BARBECUES
The Book of DRESSINGS & MARINADES
The Book of CHINESE COOKING
The Book of CAKE DECORATING
The Book of MEXICAN FOODS
The Book of ANTIPASTI
The Book of THAI COOKING
The Book of CHILDREN'S FOODS
The Book of AFTERNOON TEA
The Book of GREEK COOKING
The Book of TAPAS AND SPANISH COOKING
The Book of CLAYPOT COOKING
The Book of VEGETARIAN COOKING

INTRODUCTION

Chicken, as well as being a healthy alternative to red meat, is incredibly versatile – it can be cooked in dozens of interesting ways, and combines well with a whole host of other ingredients.

The Book of Chicken Dishes is an exciting collection of over 100 recipes, some new and exotic, others classic, traditional and everyday, all equally delicious and easy to prepare. Each recipe is illustrated in full colour with step-by-step instructions. Many of the recipes call for chicken pieces and, although they are readily available you may like to joint a chicken yourself so you have the carcass for making stock: the book starts with step-by-step directions showing how to do this.

Recipes reflect the distinctive flavours of Far Eastern, Mexican-American and European cooking, starting with Soups & Starters and followed by Canapés & Finger Food, Salads, Snacks, Classical Dishes, Tex-Mex & Far Eastern Dishes, Casseroles & Pies and European Dishes. There are quick and simple low-fat recipes for everyday eating, and when you want to entertain, chicken is perfect combined with wine and cream or fruit, herbs or spices for a delicious dinner party dish.

JOINTING A CHICKEN

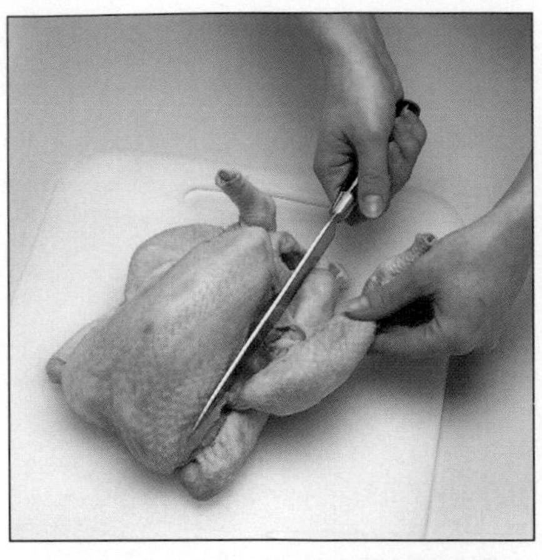

Pull the legs away from the chicken carcass and cut through the skin.

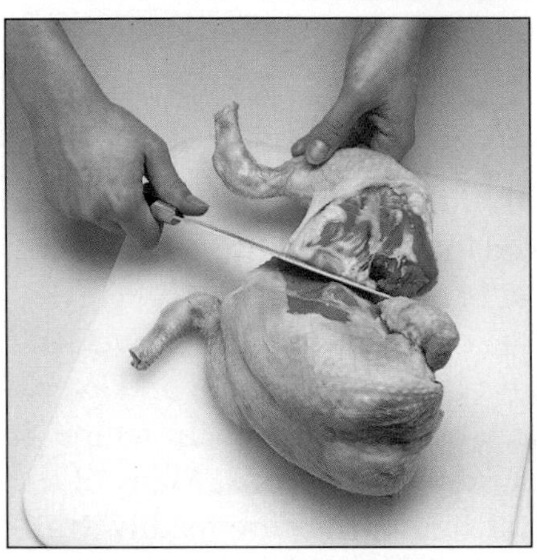

Bend the leg back to break the bone and cut through the socket. Repeat on the other side.

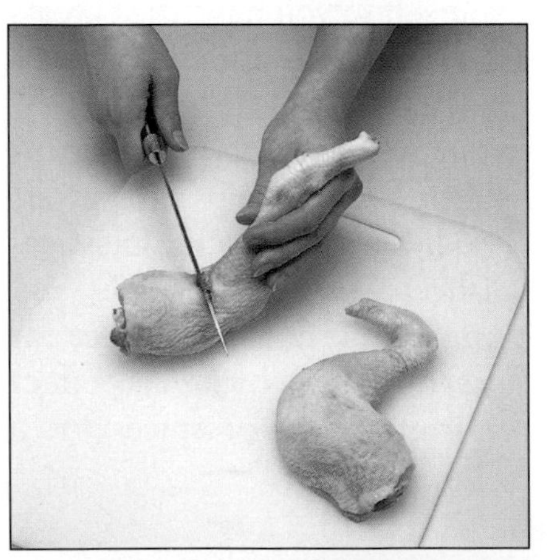

Hold the drumstick and cut through the socket to separate it from the thigh, cut the knuckle off the drumsticks.

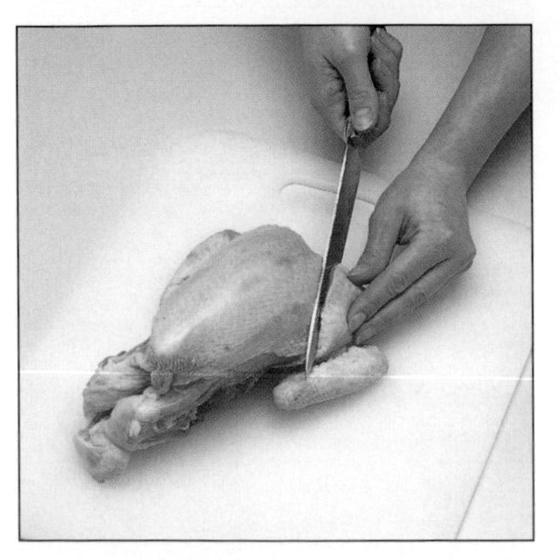

Pinch the lump of breast meat nearest to the wing, slice down and remove the wing completely.

Cut off the wing tip and fold the breast meat over the joint. Repeat with the other side.

Cut along the rib cage to separate the breast from the base of the carcass. You can use poultry shears to do this if you have them.

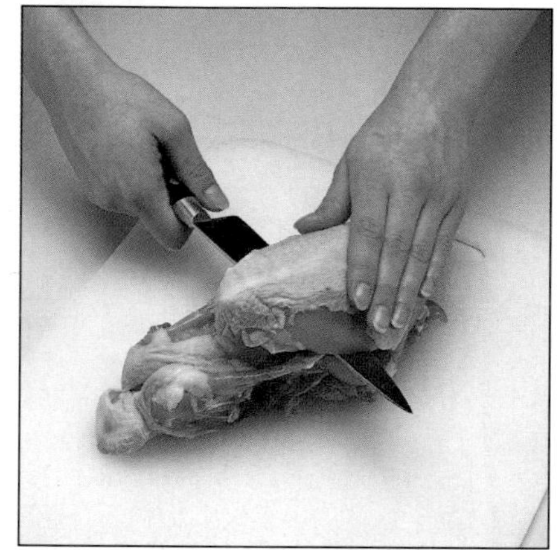

Cut the breast in half either lengthways or diagonally to give 2 breast portions.

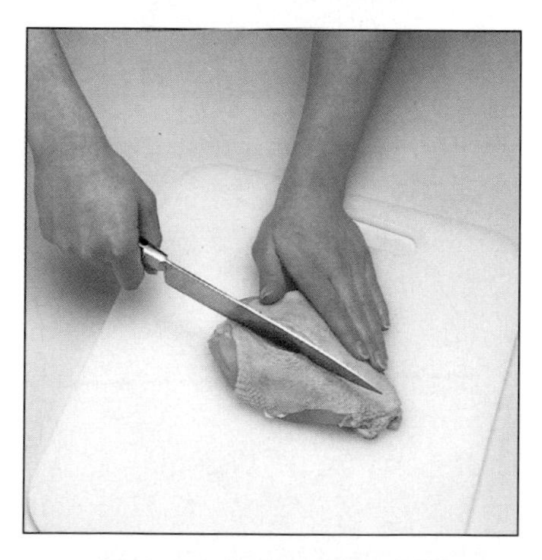

The chicken is now in 8 portions. Recipes in this book which specify skinned and boned chicken breasts are using breast portions weighing about 115 g (4 oz) unless specified otherwise.

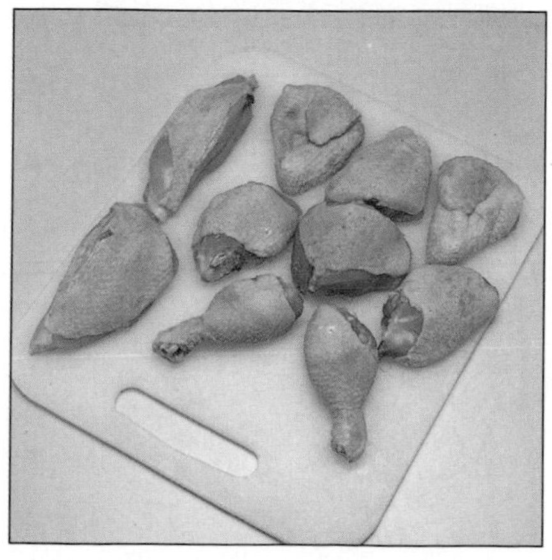

CONSOMMÉ

1.2 litres (40 fl oz/5 cups) homemade chicken stock (see Note)
115 g (4 oz) raw chicken breast
2 large eggs
4 tablespoons finely chopped fresh parsley
salt and pepper
1 teaspoon vegetable oil

Put the stock in a large pan and bring to the boil. In a blender or food processor, finely chop chicken. Separate 1 of the eggs and beat the white with a fork. Crush the shell. Mix together chicken, egg white, shell and 3 tablespoons parsley. Add to the stock.

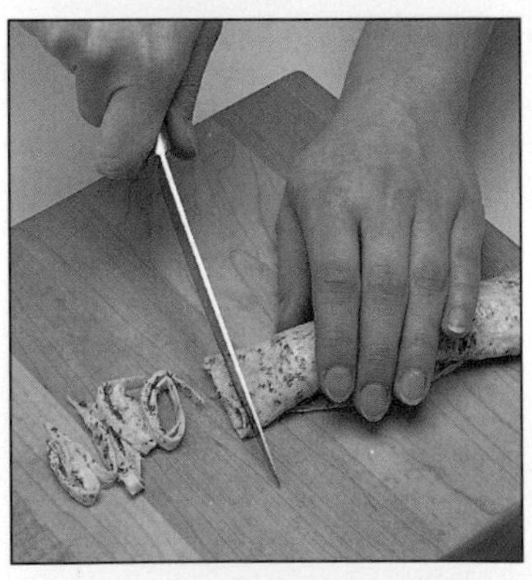

Bring stock to just below boiling point, stirring. Lower heat and simmer very gently for 25 minutes. Beat remaining egg with remaining yolk and parsley and season with salt and pepper. In a small omelette pan, heat the oil, pour in the egg mixture and cook until set. Turn out and roll up like a Swiss roll, then cut into thin strips. Strain soup through a sieve lined with muslin or cheesecloth, pour into bowls and add strips of omelette.

Serves 4.

Note: To make your own stock, put a raw or cooked chicken carcass, 1 quartered large onion, 2 halved carrots, 2 halved leeks, 2 sliced celery sticks, 1 bay leaf, some parsley stalks, 1 bunch of thyme and 6 peppercorns in a large pan with enough cold water to cover. Bring to the boil, then reduce heat and simmer for 2-3 hours. Skim off any scum. Strain into a large bowl and cool as quickly as possible. Chill in the refrigerator, then remove any fat that has set on the surface. Use within 2-3 days or freeze in convenient amounts.

THE BOOK OF
GRILLING & BARBECUES
CECILIA NORMAN

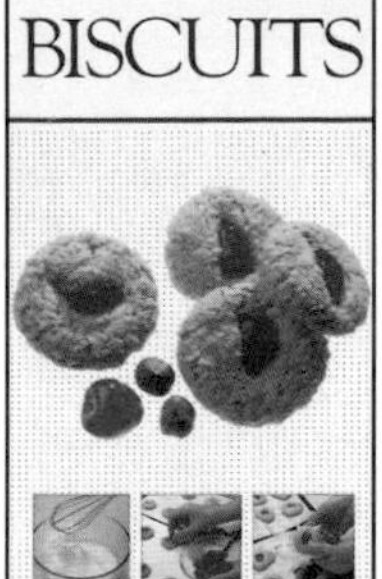
THE BOOK OF
BISCUITS
PAT ALBUREY

THE BOOK OF
SOUPS
LORNA RHODES

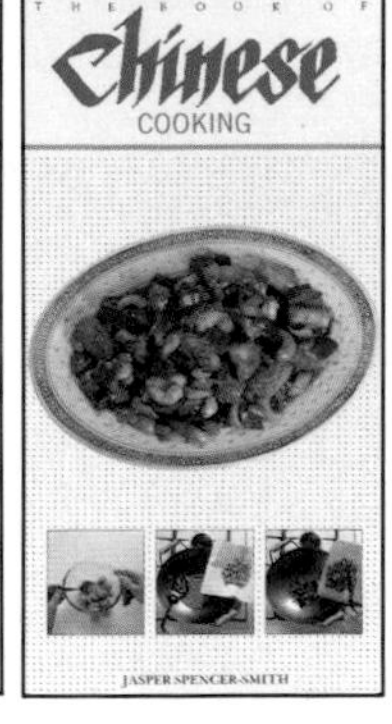
THE BOOK OF
Chinese
COOKING
JASPER SPENCER-SMITH

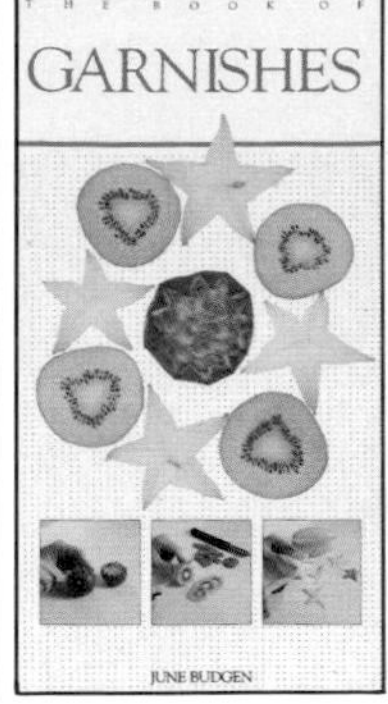
THE BOOK OF
GARNISHES
JUNE BUDGEN

THE BOOK OF
PIZZAS
AND ITALIAN BREADS
SARAH BUSH

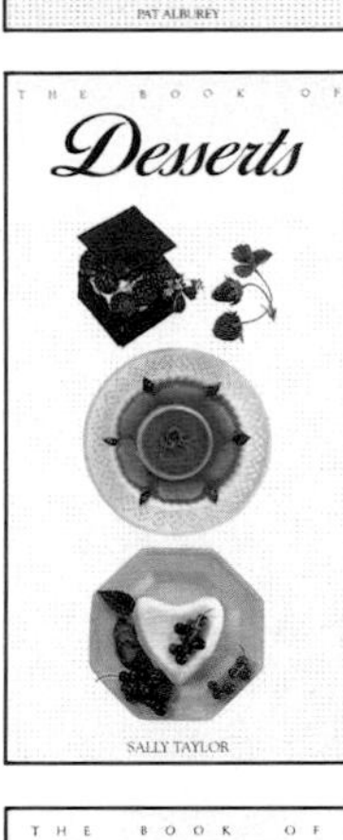
THE BOOK OF
Desserts
SALLY TAYLOR

THE BOOK OF
CHICKEN
DISHES
KERENZA HARRIES & JO CRAIG

THE BOOK OF
GIFTS
From the Pantry
ANNETTE GRIMSDALE

THE BOOK OF
CHRISTMAS FOODS
JANICE MURFITT

THE BOOK OF
BREAKFASTS & BRUNCHES
KERENZA HARRIES

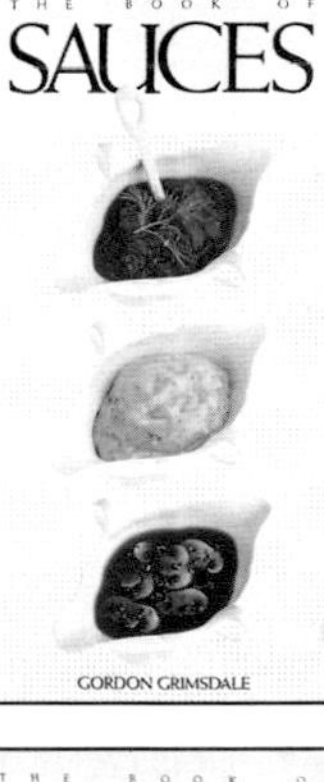
THE BOOK OF
SAUCES
GORDON GRIMSDALE

THE BOOK OF
TAPAS
AND SPANISH COOKING
HILAIRE WALDEN

THE BOOK OF
SALADS
LORNA RHODES

THE BOOK OF
PRESERVES
JAMS · CHUTNEYS · PICKLES · JELLIES
MARY NORWAK

THE BOOK OF
SANDWICHES
LOUISE STEELE

THE BOOK OF
CHILDREN'S FOODS
LORNA RHODES

THE BOOK OF
DRESSINGS & MARINADES
JANICE MURFITT

THE BOOK OF
VEGETARIAN
COOKING
LOUISE PICKFORD
THE BOOK OF
LIGHT DESSERTS
ANNE SHEASBY

THE BOOK OF
CLAYPOT
COOKING
BRIDGET JONES

THE BOOK OF
AFTERNOON
Tea
LESLEY MACKLEY

THE BOOK OF
Cake Decorating
WENDY DUFALL

THE BOOK OF
CURRIES & INDIAN FOODS
LINDA FRASER

THE BOOK OF
Mexican
FOODS
CHRISTINE BARRETT

TITLES IN THIS SERIES

Available from all good bookshops

If you have any comments to make regarding individual titles or the series, or if you have difficulty in obtaining the title you want, please write to:
Salamander Books Ltd., CS1,
129/137 York Way,
London N7 9LG

THE BOOK OF MEDITERRANEAN COOKING
LESLEY MACKLEY

THE BOOK OF ONE-POT COOKING
MARY READER

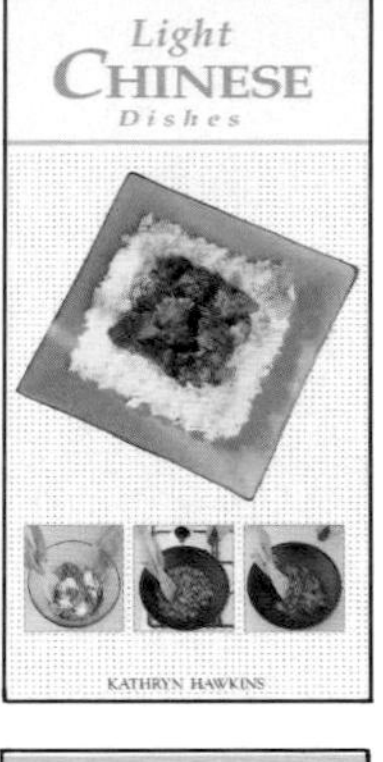

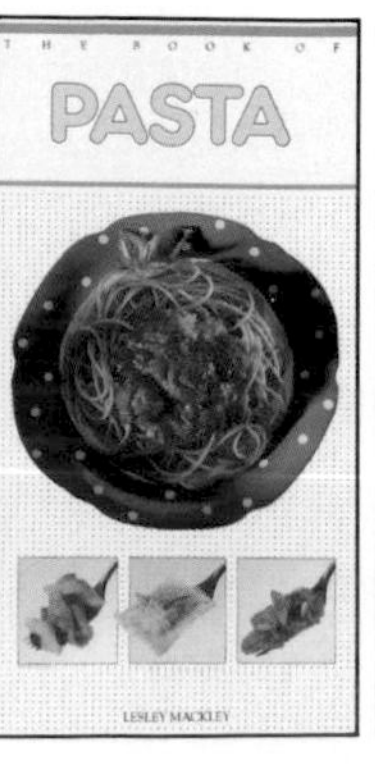

HOT & SOUR SOUP

25 g (1 oz) dried Chinese mushrooms
850 ml (30 fl oz/3¾ cups) chicken stock
25 g (1 oz) egg thread noodles, roughly crushed
115 g (4 oz) cooked chicken, shredded
1 stick celery, thinly sliced
2 small red chillies, deseeded and sliced
2 teaspoons sugar
2 tablespoons cider vinegar
pinch of white pepper
3 tablespoons dark soy sauce
1 tablespoon cornflour
1 egg
3 teaspoons sesame oil
2 spring onions, finely chopped
1 tablespoon finely chopped coriander

Soak the mushrooms in 300 ml (10 fl oz/1¼ cups) of the stock for 20 minutes, then drain, reserving any soaking liquor. Squeeze out any excess liquid and finely shred the mushrooms. Soak the noodles in the mushroom liquor for 5 minutes. Bring all the stock and the reserved soaking liquor to the boil and add the chicken, mushrooms, noodles, celery, chillies, sugar, vinegar, pepper and 2 tablespoons of the soy sauce and simmer together for 2 minutes.

Blend the cornflour with the remaining soy sauce and pour into the soup, stirring well, and continue to simmer for a further 2 minutes. Beat the egg with the sesame oil and pour into the simmering soup in a fine stream, whisking with a fork as you pour. Stir in the onions and coriander and serve at once.

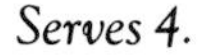

Serves 4.

CREAM OF CHICKEN SOUP

25 g (1oz/6 teaspoons) butter
1 small leek, washed and diced
45 g (1½ oz/¼ cup, plus 6 teaspoons) plain flour
850 ml (30 fl oz/3¾ cups) chicken stock
150 ml (5 fl oz/⅔ cup) dry white wine
115 g (4 oz) cooked chicken, finely chopped
pinch of ground nutmeg
150 ml (5 fl oz/⅔ cup) single (light) cream
2 teaspoons chopped fresh chives
150 ml (5 fl oz/⅔ cup) thick sour cream and croûtons, to serve

In a saucepan, melt the butter and gently sauté the leek until soft. Stir in the flour and cook over a low heat for 1-2 minutes.

Remove the pan from the heat and slowly add the stock, a little at a time, stirring well. Return to the heat and bring to the boil, stirring until thickened.

Add the wine, cover and simmer gently for 15 minutes; add the chicken and nutmeg and simmer for a further 5 minutes. Pour in the cream and heat gently without boiling, then stir in the chopped chives. Serve in warmed bowls with spoonfuls of thick sour cream and croûtons.

Serves 4.

CORN & PRAWN CHOWDER

425 ml (15 fl oz/2 cups) milk
425 ml (15 fl oz/2 cups) chicken stock
350 g (12 oz) sweetcorn kernels
25 g (1 oz/6 teaspoons) butter
1 small onion, finely chopped
2 teaspoons plain flour
225 g (8 oz) raw potatoes, cubed
175 g (6 oz) cooked chicken, diced
175 g (6 oz) cooked peeled prawns
2 tablespoons chopped fresh parsley
salt and pepper
55 g (2oz/¼ cup) grated Cheddar cheese

Mix together the milk and the chicken stock in a jug.

In a blender or food processor, blend 175 g (6 oz) sweetcorn in a little of the milk mixture until smooth, then add the remaining liquor. In a pan, melt the butter and fry the onion until softened, stir in the flour and cook for 1 minute. Remove from the heat and stir in the sweetcorn mixture, a little at a time, stirring well between each addition.

Return to the heat and bring to the boil, stirring continuously. Add the potatoes and simmer gently for 15 minutes. Stir in the remaining sweetcorn, chicken, prawns and parsley and season to taste. Sprinkle with the grated cheese and serve with warm crusty bread.

Serves 4.

COCK-A-LEEKIE SOUP

6 skinned chicken thighs
1 litre (35 fl oz/4½ cups) chicken stock
3 leeks

Place the chicken thighs in a large pan with the chicken stock and simmer gently for 35-40 minutes.

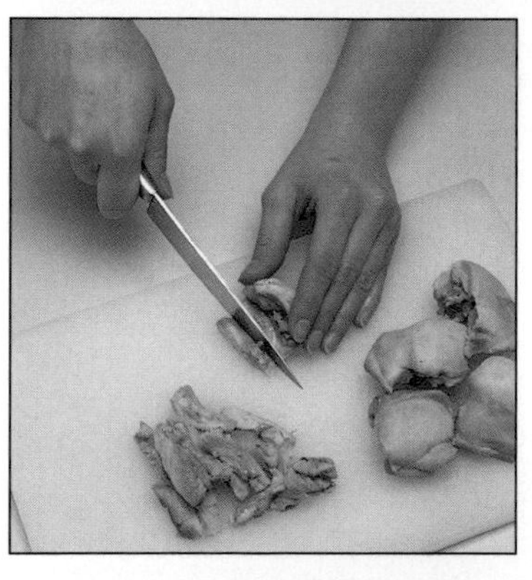

Meanwhile, trim the leeks and slice into rings. Remove the cooked chicken from the stock with a slotted spoon. Remove the meat from the bones and cut into bite-sized pieces. Put to one side.

Increase the heat and bring the stock to a fast simmer. Add the prepared leeks and cook for 3-4 minutes until the leeks are just tender. Add the chicken to the pan and simmer for 2-3 minutes. Serve hot with warm rolls.

Serves 4.

Variation: Add 12 ready-to-eat stoned and quartered prunes with the chicken in Step 3.

CHICKEN SOUP WITH KREPLACH

225 g (8 oz/2 cups) plain flour
salt and pepper
3 eggs, beaten
2 tablespoons chopped fresh parsley
2 tablespoons chopped fresh oregano
1 tablespoon oil
1 small onion, finely chopped
175 g (6 oz) skinned and boned chicken, minced
finely grated rind of 1 lemon
2 tablespoons Greek yogurt
550 ml (20 fl oz/2½ cups) Consommé (see page 10)

Sift the flour and a pinch of salt into a bowl and make a well in the centre. Add the eggs and 1 tablespoon each of parsley and oregano.

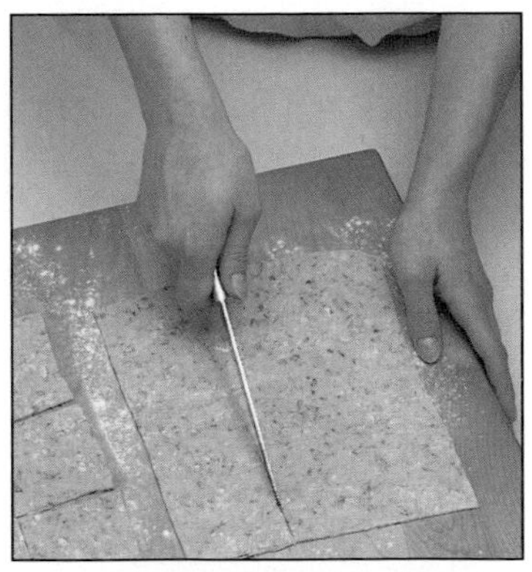

Using a fork, gradually blend in the flour to form a soft dough. If the dough is too sticky, add a little more flour. Knead the dough on a lightly floured surface for 3-4 minutes. Wrap in plastic wrap and refrigerate for 30 minutes. In small pan, heat the oil. Add the onion and cook until soft. Add the chicken and cook for a further 2-3 minutes. Add the lemon rind, remaining herbs and yogurt. Season and put on one side to cool. On a floured board, roll out the dough to about 0.3 cm (⅛ in) thickness. Cut the dough into 5-6 cm (2-2½ in) squares.

Place a spoonful of the filling on each square, brush the edges with a little water and fold the dough in half over the filling to make a triangle. Pinch the edges together to seal, then pull 2 corners together and pinch them to make them stick. Repeat with the remaining dough and filling. Bring a pan of salted water to the boil and cook the kreplach for 5-7 minutes or until the dough is cooked. Heat the consommé, add the kreplach, heat through and serve.

Serves 4.

CHICKEN & PRAWN QUENELLES

350 g (12 oz) skinned and boned chicken breasts
salt and pepper
2 egg whites
150 ml (5 fl oz/⅔ cup) double (thick) cream
115 g (4 oz) cooked peeled prawns, chopped
55 g (2 oz) smoked salmon, chopped
300 ml (10 fl oz/1¼ cups) chicken stock
4 tablespoons crème fraîche
1 teaspoon cornflour mixed with 1 tablespoon chicken stock
finely grated rind and juice of ½ lemon
3 teaspoons chopped fresh dill

Put the chicken in a blender or food processor and mince finely.

With the motor running, add the salt and pepper, egg whites and cream. Process again for a few seconds (making sure you do not overbeat the mousse). Transfer to a bowl and gently fold in the prawns and smoked salmon. Leave to chill for 30 minutes. Bring the stock to a simmer. Using 2 dessertspoons, shape the mixture into neat quenelles and slide into the stock. Poach for 1-2 minutes until firm to touch. Carefully remove with a slotted spoon. Transfer to a dish, cover with buttered foil and keep warm while cooking the remaining mixture.

Increase the heat under the stock and boil rapidly until the stock is reduced by half. Add the crème fraîche and the cornflour mixed with the stock and, stirring all the time, simmer the sauce until it thickens. Add the lemon rind and juice and season with a little salt and pepper. Add the chopped dill. Pour the sauce over the quenelles and serve hot.

Serves 4.

RICOTTA-STUFFED MUSHROOMS

3 tablespoons olive oil
2 shallots, finely chopped
175 g (6 oz) skinned and boned chicken breast
115 g (4 oz) ricotta cheese
4 tablespoons grated Parmesan cheese
8 black olives, chopped
55 g (2 oz/½ cup) chopped pine nuts
2 tablespoons chopped fresh basil
¼ teaspoon freshly grated nutmeg
salt and pepper
8 open cup mushrooms

In a pan, heat 1 tablespoon oil and fry the shallots gently until soft and transparent. Remove from the heat and set aside.

Preheat oven to 230C (450F/Gas 8). In a food processor, finely process the chicken breast and transfer to a bowl. Add the ricotta cheese, 3 tablespoons Parmesan, olives, pine nuts, basil, shallots and nutmeg and season with a little salt and pepper.

Put the mushrooms, stalk-ends up, in an ovenproof dish and fill each one with the chicken mixture. Sprinkle over the remaining oil and Parmesan cheese and bake for 10-12 minutes or until golden. Serve hot.

Serves 4.

CHICKEN MOUSSELINES

350 g (12 oz) skinned and boned chicken breasts
25 g (1 oz/6 teaspoons) butter, softened
1 large egg, beaten
150 ml (5 fl oz/⅔ cup) double (thick) cream
1 tablespoon chopped fresh chives
1 teaspoon finely grated lemon rind
salt and pepper
FILLING:
78 g (2¾ oz) pepper full fat soft cheese
2 teaspoons lemon juice
SAUCE:
2 red peppers (capsicums), deseeded and halved
25 g (1 oz) sun-dried tomatoes in oil, drained
3 tablespoons Greek yogurt
1 teaspoon red wine vinegar

Place the chicken and butter into a blender or food processor and process until smooth. With the blades running, pour in the egg and 85 ml (3 fl oz) of the cream. Stir in the chives, lemon rind and seasoning and spoon into six 115 ml (4 fl oz/½ cup) capacity moulds, tapping them well on the worktop to level the surface. For the filling, cream together the soft cheese, the remaining 55 ml (2 fl oz) cream and the lemon juice and put into a large piping bag fitted with a large plain nozzle.

Plunge the piping nozzle deep into the centre of the filled moulds and pipe one-quarter of the filling into each; use a wet finger to smooth the chicken back over the filling where the nozzle has been. Cover each with a small round of baking parchment and place in a shallow pan half-filled with boiling water. Cover and simmer for 15 minutes.

Preheat grill. For the sauce, place the pepper (capsicum) halves under a very hot grill and cook until the skins are blackened, allow to cool and peel.

In a blender or food processor, process the peppers (capsicums), tomatoes, yogurt and vinegar until smooth, then pour into a pan and heat gently. Pour some sauce into 6 individual side plates, remove the chicken mousselines from the pan and drain off any excess liquid which has collected in the moulds.

Peel off the baking parchment and tip the mousselines on top of the sauce. Serve at once, garnished with herbs. Serve any extra sauce separately.

Serves 6.

CHICKEN & HAM MOUSSE

175 g (6 oz) cooked chicken, finely minced
115 g (4 oz) cooked ham, finely minced
1 tablespoon lemon juice
1 tablespoon chopped fresh parsley
1 tablespoon chopped fresh chives
150 ml (5 fl oz/⅔ cup) mayonnaise
2 teaspoons powdered gelatine
3 tablespoons chicken stock
150 ml (5 fl oz/⅔ cup) double (thick) cream

In a bowl, mix the chicken with the ham, lemon juice, chopped herbs and mayonnaise.

In a small pan, sprinkle the gelatine over the chicken stock and leave for 5 minutes to soften. Melt very gently over a low heat until gelatine dissolves, then cool and fold into the ham and chicken mixture.

Lightly beat the cream to form soft peaks and then carefully fold into the chicken and ham mixture. Pour the mixture into a 1 litre (35 fl oz/4½ cups) mould and leave to set in the refrigerator for 2-3 hours. Unmould carefully and garnish with fresh herbs. Serve with hot crusty rolls.

Serves 4.

-HOT CHICKEN LIVER MOUSSES-

225 g (8 oz) chicken livers
2 eggs
300 ml (10 fl oz/1¼ cups) single (light) cream
salt and pepper
1 tablespoon oil
2 shallots, finely chopped
½ clove garlic, crushed
200 g (7 oz) can chopped tomatoes
6 tablespoons port
3 tablespoons Madeira
2 teaspoons tomato purée (paste)
1 teaspoon sugar
150 ml (5 fl oz/⅔ cup) chicken stock
25 g (1 oz/6 teaspoons) butter

Preheat oven to 160C (325F/Gas 3). Remove the cores from the chicken livers. Chop the livers coarsely and put into a blender or food processor with the eggs, cream and salt and pepper and purée until smooth. Pour into a jug and refrigerate for 30 minutes. Half-fill a roasting tin with boiling water. Lightly grease four 150 ml (5 fl oz/⅔ cup) capacity ramekins, pour the mousse mixture into the ramekins and place in the roasting tin. Cover with greased foil and bake for 20-25 minutes until mousses are firm.

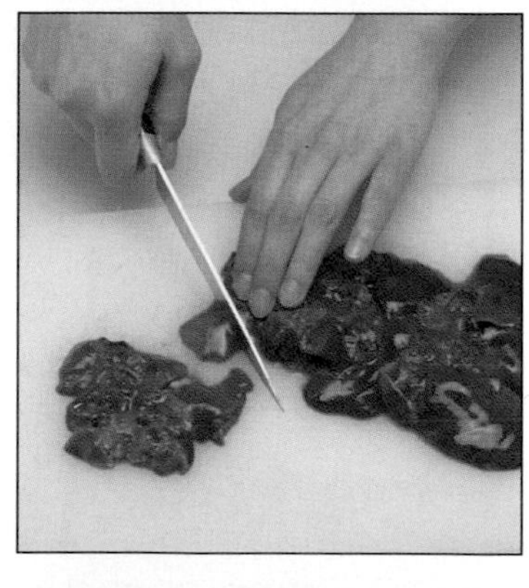

In a pan, heat the oil, add shallots and garlic and cook for 1-2 minutes. Add tomatoes and cook for a further 3-4 minutes. Add the port and Madeira and boil rapidly for 1 minute. Add the tomato purée (paste), sugar and chicken stock, season, and simmer for 10-12 minutes. Purée in a a blender or food processor, return to pan and whisk in the butter. Run a knife around the edge of each ramekin and turn onto a plate. Spoon the sauce around the mousses and serve.

Serves 4.

CHICKEN LIVER PÂTÉ

450 g (1 lb) chicken livers
225 g (8 oz/1 cup) unsalted butter
1 clove garlic, crushed
2 tablespoons brandy
2 tablespoons port
salt and pepper
2 tablespoons redcurrant jelly

Soak the livers in cold water for 1 hour, drain and remove the cores. In a frying pan, heat 25 g (1 oz/6 teaspoons) butter, add the livers and fry for 2 minutes, then add the garlic and cook for a further 2-3 minutes until the livers are cooked through, but still pink.

Cut the remaining butter into cubes and add to the pan. Remove the pan from the heat and allow the butter to melt over the livers. Meanwhile, put the brandy and port into a small pan and boil rapidly for about 1½ minutes until the liquid is reduced to a syrup; make sure you do not over reduce the liquid as it could burn and ruin the flavour of the pâté.

Add this mixture to the pan of livers, season with salt and pepper and leave the mixture to cool for 15 minutes. Put the liver mixture into a blender or food processor and blend until you have a smooth pâté. Pour into 8 individual ramekins or 1 large serving dish. Melt the redcurrant jelly and pour over the pâté. Chill for at least 3-4 hours before serving.

Serves 8.

—LAYERED COUNTRY TERRINE—

8 rashers rindless, smoked streaky bacon
115 g (4 oz) chicken livers
115 g (4 oz) minced pork
115 g (4 oz) herby sausagemeat
1 clove garlic
1 onion, finely chopped
3 tablespoons chopped fresh parsley
25 g (1 oz/½ cup) fresh white breadcrumbs
55 ml (2 fl oz/¼ cup) brandy
1 small egg, beaten
¼ teaspoon freshly grated nutmeg
1 teaspoon finely grated lemon rind
salt and pepper
2 skinned and boned chicken breasts
1 bay leaf

Preheat oven to 180C (350F/Gas 4). Place the bacon on a board and stretch with the back of a knife. Use 4 rashers to line a 1.2 litre (40 fl oz/5 cup) loaf tin, reserving 4 rashers for the top. Roughly chop the chicken livers, mix them together with the pork, sausagemeat, garlic, onion and parsley. Soak the breadcrumbs in the brandy, then add to the meat mixture with the egg, nutmeg, lemon rind and seasonings.

Spread one third of the meat mixture over the bacon in the tin. Cut the chicken into very thin slices and layer half over the meat mixture. Cover with half the remaining meat mixture, then cover with the remaining chicken and the rest of the meat mixture. Lay the reserved bacon on top and add the bay leaf. Cover with foil. Stand the terrine in a baking tin three-quarters full of boiling water. Bake for 1½ hours. Allow to cool. Serve with crusty bread, salad and spiced chutney.

Serves 4-6.

WRAPPED TERRINE

115 g (4 oz) large spinach leaves, stalks removed
115 g (4 oz) carrots, peeled
115 g (4 oz) French beans, topped and tailed
450 g (1 lb) skinned and boned chicken meat
55 g (2 oz/1 cup) fresh white breadcrumbs
85 ml (3 fl oz/⅓ cup) double (thick) cream
4 teaspoons creamed horseradish sauce
2 teaspoons lemon juice
2 tablespoons dry sherry
¼ teaspoon ground nutmeg
salt and pepper
2 eggs, separated

Preheat oven to 180C (350F/Gas 4). Blanch spinach for 30 seconds, refresh and drain well.

Cut the carrots into even-sized sticks, about the same length as the beans. Blanch the carrots and beans for 3-4 minutes in separate pans of boiling, salted water, then plunge into cold water to refresh and drain thoroughly. Put the chicken, breadcrumbs, cream, horseradish, lemon juice, sherry, nutmeg and seasoning into a blender or food processor and blend until smooth, then stir in the egg yolks and mix well.

Stiffly whisk the egg whites and fold them into the chicken mixture. Lightly oil a 1.2 litre (40 fl oz/5 cup) capacity loaf tin and line with the spinach leaves, slightly overlapping them each time and leaving enough to overhang the top rim of tin to cover the top. Spread one-third of the chicken mixture over the base of tin and level the surface.

Cover with a neat layer of carrots, top with half the remaining chicken mixture and cover with a layer of beans.

Top with the final layer of chicken mixture and fold the overhanging spinach leaves over the mixture to neaten. Cover with a piece of baking parchment and a layer of foil, then stand in a deep baking tin. Add enough boiling water to three-quarters fill the tin.

Cook in oven for 50 minutes until firm, then leave to cool. Pour off any excess juices from the tin, turn out terrine onto a serving platter and garnish with lemon twists. Serve cold with a garlic and lemon mayonnaise.

Serves 6.

—ORIENTAL CHICKEN PARCELS—

2 tablespoons dry sherry
2 tablespoons soy sauce
2 tablespoons sesame oil
350 g (12 oz) skinned and boned chicken breasts
2.5 cm (1 in) piece fresh root ginger, finely chopped
8 spring onions, finely sliced
1 stick celery, finely sliced
oil for brushing

Cut the chicken into 16 equal-sized pieces and put into a shallow dish. Mix together the sherry, soy sauce and sesame oil, pour over the chicken and leave to marinate for 45 minutes.

Cut 16 squares of kitchen foil, each large enough to wrap around a piece of chicken and brush each square of foil with a little oil. Put a piece of chicken on each piece of foil and top with a little of the ginger, spring onion and celery. Spoon over any remaining marinade and fold the foil over to make parcels, making sure the edges are well sealed.

Place the parcels in a bamboo or metal steamer and cook for 10 minutes or until the chicken is cooked through. Serve in the foil.

Serves 4.

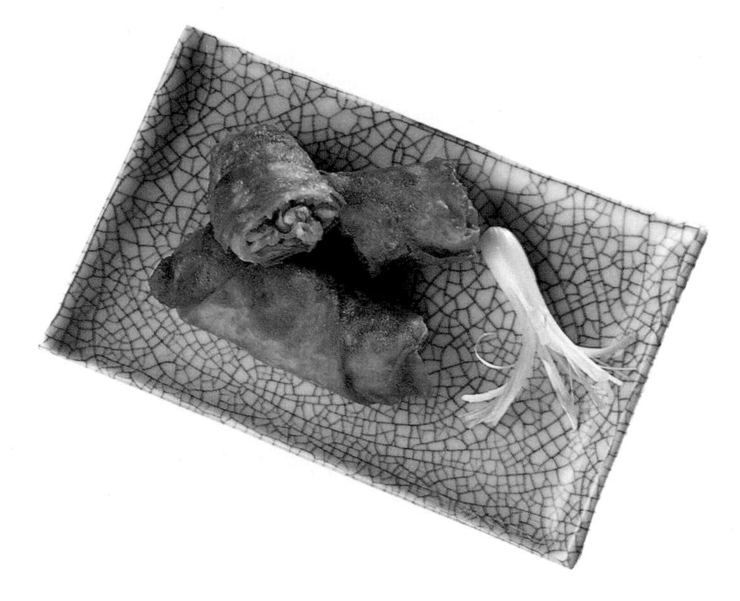

SPRING ROLLS

2 tablespoons vegetable oil
1 clove garlic, finely chopped
2.5 cm (1 in) piece fresh root ginger, finely chopped
115 g (4 oz) chicken breast, shredded
55 g (2 oz) mange tout (snow peas), finely sliced
175 g (6 oz) shiitake mushrooms, sliced
8 spring onions, finely chopped
55 g (2 oz) cooked peeled prawns, chopped
1 tablespoon soy sauce
1 teaspoon sesame oil
300 g (10 oz) filo pastry
1 egg white, for brushing
oil for deep frying
bottled chilli and hoisin sauces, to serve

In wok or large frying pan, heat the oil, add the garlic and ginger and stir-fry for 15 seconds, then add the chicken breast and continue cooking for 2-3 minutes. Add the mange tout (snow peas), mushrooms, spring onions and prawns, followed by the soy sauce and sesame oil. Mix well and transfer to a bowl to cool. Cut the filo pastry into sixteen 17.5 cm (7 in) squares. On a board, place one square of pastry diagonally towards you and cover with another square of pastry to give 2 layers.

Place a large tablespoon of mixture just below the centre of the pastry. Fold the bottom corner over and then the 2 side flaps to give an elongated open envelope. Brush with egg white and roll up, pressing gently. Repeat with the remaining filo pastry and filling. Half-fill a deep fat pan or fryer with oil and heat to 190C (375F). Fry the rolls, in 2 batches, for about 4 minutes or until golden Leave to drain on absorbent kitchen paper. Serve with chilli and hoisin sauces.

Serves 4.

CHICKEN APRICOT FILOS

½ tablespoon oil for frying, plus extra for brushing
½ onion, finely chopped
55 g (2 oz/½ cup) dried apricots, finely chopped
100 g (4 oz) cooked chicken, finely diced
4 tablespoons Greek yogurt
2 tablespoons chopped fresh coriander
salt and pepper
3 sheets filo pastry

Preheat oven to 190C (375F/Gas 5). In a small pan, heat the oil, add the onion and cook gently for 3-4 minutes without browning. Add the dried apricots and cook for a further 2 minutes.

Put the onion mixture into a bowl, add the chicken, yogurt, coriander and salt and pepper and mix well. Cut each sheet of filo pastry in half, then cut each half into 4 to form sixteen 10 cm (4 in) squares.

Brush each square with a little oil and place a spoonful of the chicken mixture in the centre. Gather up the corners of the filo pastry and pinch together to form a loose bag. Place the filo bags on 2 greased baking sheets and bake for 10-12 minutes or until the pastry is crisp and golden. Serve warm.

Makes 16.

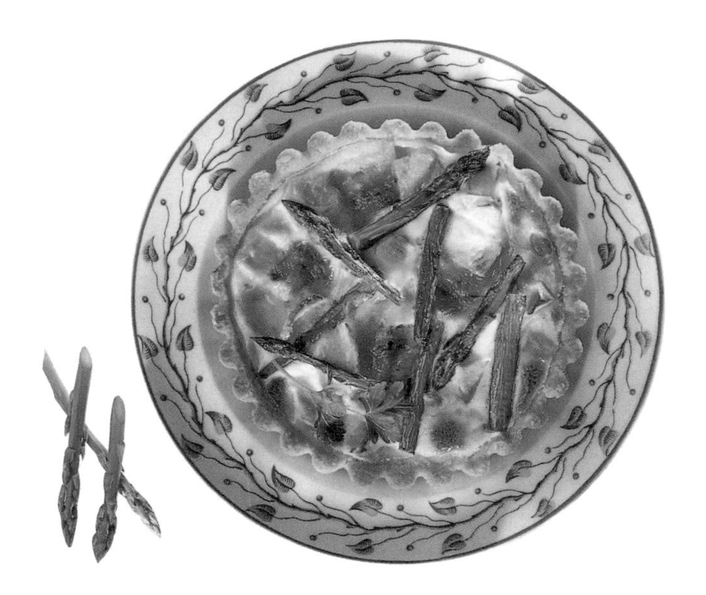

CHICKEN & BRIE TARTS

85 g (3 oz/¾ cup) plain flour
45 g (1½ oz/6 teaspoons) rice flour
4 teaspoons grated Parmesan cheese
1 teaspoon dry mustard powder
85 g (3 oz/⅓ cup) butter, diced
1 egg yolk
FOR THE FILLING:
115 g (4 oz) cooked chicken, diced
115 g (4 oz) blue brie, diced
16 asparagus sprue
1 large egg
115 ml (4 fl oz/½ cup) single (light) cream
salt and pepper

Preheat oven to 200C (400F/Gas 6). To make the pastry, place the flour, rice flour, Parmesan, mustard and butter in a food processor and blend for 45 seconds. Add the egg yolk and 2 teaspoons cold water and blend until the pastry binds together, adding a little more water, if necessary. Wrap in a polythene bag and set aside to relax in the refrigerator for 15-20 minutes. Divide the pastry into 4, roll out on a floured surface and use to line four 11 cm (4½ in) diameter, individual, loose-based flan tins.

Arrange the chicken and brie over the base of each flan. Blanch the asparagus in boiling, salted water for 2 minutes, drain and refresh under cold running water and pat dry on absorbent kitchen paper. Cut the asparagus in half and arrange over the chicken mixture. Beat together the egg, cream and seasoning and divide equally among the tarts. Bake in the oven for 25 minutes until firm and set.

Serves 4.

NUTTY GOUJONS

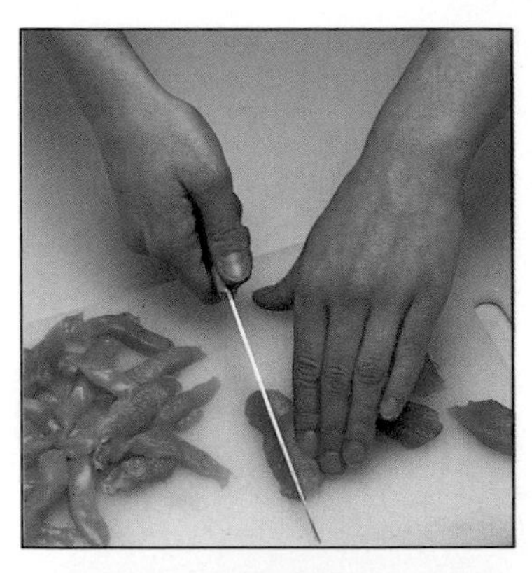

350 g (12 oz) skinned and boned chicken breasts
55 g (2 oz/½ cup) ground almonds
115 g (4 oz/2 cups) fresh white breadcrumbs
2 teaspoons finely chopped fresh parsley
25 g (1 oz/¼ cup) plain flour
salt and pepper
1 large egg, beaten
oil for deep frying
2 tablespoons spiced plum chutney
1 tablespoon mayonnaise
1 teaspoon finely grated orange rind
3 teaspoons orange juice

Cut chicken into thin strips. Mix together the almonds, breadcrumbs and parsley.

Put the flour, salt and pepper and chicken into a large polythene bag and shake well. Dip the chicken strips into the beaten egg, then roll in the breadcrumb mixture to coat completely. Chill in the freezer for 15-20 minutes. Half-fill a deep fat pan or fryer with oil and heat to 190C (375F) or until a cube of day-old bread browns in 40 seconds. Fry the chicken strips, a few at a time, for 3-4 minutes until golden. Drain on absorbent kitchen paper and keep warm while cooking the remaining goujons.

Mix together the spiced plum chutney, mayonnaise, orange rind and juice and spoon into a small dish. Serve the goujons with the sauce for dipping.

Serves 4.

DEVILLED CHICKEN WINGS

1 tablespoon vegetable oil
1 onion, chopped
1 clove garlic, crushed
2.5 cm (1 in) fresh root ginger, peeled and chopped
½ teaspoon cayenne pepper
½ teaspoon paprika
3 tablespoons red wine vinegar
85 ml (3 fl oz/⅓ cup) tomato ketchup (sauce)
2 tablespoons brown sugar
2 tablespoons hot pepper or chilli sauce
2 teaspoons Dijon mustard
16 chicken wings

Heat the oil, cook onion, garlic and ginger until soft. Add the cayenne and paprika.

Cook for 1 minute, stirring. Add the vinegar, tomato ketchup (sauce), brown sugar, chilli sauce and the mustard and simmer for 4-5 minutes. Preheat grill.

Arrange the chicken wings in a shallow ovenproof dish or roasting tin – do not pack them too tightly. Pour over the sauce and cook the chicken wings under the hot grill for 12-15 minutes, turning and basting frequently with the sauce until crisp, brown and sticky.

Serves 4.

ORIENTAL BACON ROLLS

225 g (8 oz) chicken livers
2 teaspoons soy sauce
1 teaspoon finely chopped fresh root ginger
6 teaspoons clear honey
4 teaspoons dry sherry
8 rashers streaky bacon
8 canned water chestnuts, drained

Soak the chicken livers in cold water for 1 hour, drain and remove the cores. Cut the livers into 16 pieces.

Mix together the soy sauce, ginger, 2 teaspoons honey and sherry. Add the prepared chicken livers and leave to marinate for 25 minutes. Preheat grill. Remove the rinds from the bacon. Using the back of a knife, stretch each rasher of bacon and cut in half.

Cut the water chestnuts in half, place at the end of a rasher of bacon, top with a piece of liver and roll up in the bacon. Secure with a wooden cocktail stick. Continue until all the ingredients are used. Place the bacon rolls in a frying pan or roasting tin, pour over the remaining marinade and drizzle with the remaining honey. Place under the hot grill and cook until the bacon is crisp and brown and the honey has caramelised.

Makes 16.

SPINACH ROULADE

15 g (½ oz/3 teaspoons) garlic and herb-flavoured butter
225 g (8 oz) frozen spinach, thawed and drained
salt and pepper
freshly grated nutmeg
2 large eggs, separated
2 tablespoons grated Parmesan cheese
FOR THE FILLING:
4 tablespoons mayonnaise
1 tablespoon creamed horseradish sauce
175 g (6 oz) smoked chicken, finely shredded
1 teaspoon finely grated lemon rind
1 large red pepper (capsicum), deseeded, skinned and chopped

Preheat oven to 200C (400F/Gas 6). Grease a 30 x 23 cm (12 x 9 in) Swiss roll tin and line with greased greaseproof paper. In a saucepan, melt the butter, add the spinach and cook for 1 minute, then season with salt and pepper and freshly grated nutmeg. Purée the mixture in a blender or food processor. Beat in the egg yolks. Stiffly whisk the egg whites and gently fold into the spinach mixture. Spoon into the prepared tin and level the surface. Bake in the oven for 7-10 minutes until well risen and springy to the touch.

Sprinkle the Parmesan over a large piece of baking parchment. Turn the roulade out onto the baking parchment, remove the lining paper, trim the edges and roll up loosely. Allow to cool. Mix together the mayonnaise, horseradish, chicken, lemon rind and chopped pepper (capsicum). Unroll the roulade, spread with the chicken filling and re-roll. Serve cut into slices.

Serves 4.

– CHICKEN & MANGO YAKITORI –

3 large skinned and boned chicken breasts, weighing about 175 g (6 oz) each
1 large ripe mango
70 ml (2½ fl oz/⅓ cup) chicken stock
70 ml (2½ fl oz/⅓ cup) sake or sweet white wine
85 ml (3 fl oz/⅓ cup) dark soy sauce
1½ tablespoons brown sugar
30 ml (1 fl oz/6 teaspoons) sweet sherry
1 clove garlic, crushed

Cut the chicken into long, thin strips about 0.5 cm (¼ in) wide. Peel and stone the mango and cut the flesh into 2 cm (¾ in) pieces. Thread a strip of chicken onto a skewer, followed by a piece of mango.

Wrap the chicken over the mango, then thread another piece of mango onto the skewer and continue threading the ingredients in this way so that the chicken weaves over and under the mango. Place all the remaining ingredients in a small pan and heat gently until the sugar has dissolved, then bring to the boil for 1 minute. Set aside to cool. Preheat grill.

Put a small amount of the sauce aside to use as a dip. Brush a little of the remaining sauce over the kebabs. Place under the hot grill for 30 seconds, then brush with a little more sauce and return to the grill and cook for a further 30 seconds. Repeat this process for 2-3 minutes or until the kebabs are cooked. Serve hot.

Makes 16-20.

CHICKEN SATAY

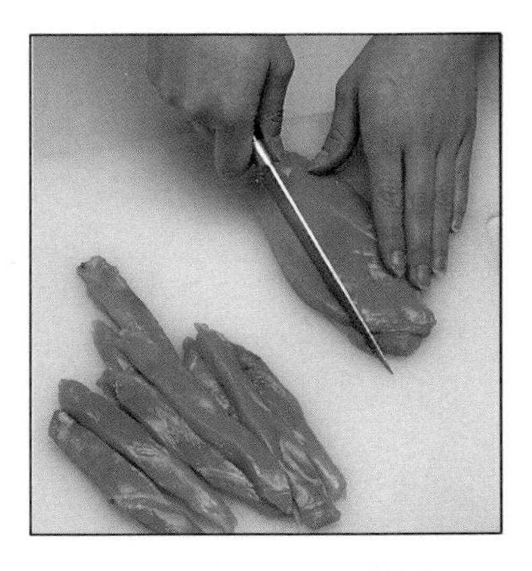

1 tablespoon grated fresh root ginger
1 teaspoon ground coriander
1 teaspoon turmeric
½ teaspoon chilli powder
1 teaspoon brown sugar
2 tablespoons light soy sauce
2 tablespoons seasame oil
2 cloves garlic, crushed
juice of 1 lime
350 g (12 oz) skinned and boned chicken breasts, cut into long, thin strips
85 g (3 oz) onion, chopped
55 g (2 oz) creamed coconut
1 teaspoon chilli powder
150 ml (5 fl oz/⅔ cup) boiling water
55 g (2 oz/3 tablespoons) crunchy peanut butter

In a blender or food processor, blend together the ginger, coriander, turmeric, chilli, sugar, soy sauce, 1 tablespoon sesame oil, garlic and the lime juice; pour over the chicken strips and leave to marinate for 3-4 hours. To make the sauce, sauté half the onion in the remaining sesame oil until soft.

In a blender or food processor, blend the remaining half of the onion, creamed coconut and chilli powder with the boiling water. Add this paste to the sautéed onion, stir in the peanut butter and 2 tablespoons of the marinade, bring to the boil and simmer for 5 minutes until thickened. Preheat grill. Thread the chicken onto skewers and cook under the hot grill for 15-20 minutes turning frequently. Serve with the peanut sauce for dipping.

Serves 4.

CLUB SANDWICH

12 slices white or brown bread
a little butter or margarine, for spreading
12 rashers streaky bacon, rinds removed
350 g (12 oz) cooked chicken breasts, thinly sliced
6 tablespoons mayonnaise
freshly ground black pepper
3 tomatoes, sliced
½ iceburg lettuce, shredded

Toast the bread on both sides and spread one side with a little butter or margarine; keep warm. Grill the bacon until crispy and leave to drain on kitchen paper; keep warm. Mix together the chicken and mayonnaise.

To assemble the sandwich, place 4 slices of toast, buttered-sides up, on a board. Spoon on the chicken and spread evenly. Season with a little black pepper and top each with another slice of toast, buttered sides up.

To make the second layer, cover each sandwich with 3 slices of bacon, some sliced tomato and a little shredded lettuce. Season again with black pepper and top with the 4 remaining slices of toast, buttered-sides down. Insert 2 cocktail sticks into each sandwich, at opposite corners to help hold the sandwich together. Carefully slice between the cocktail sticks to cut the sandwich neatly into quarters.

Serves 4.

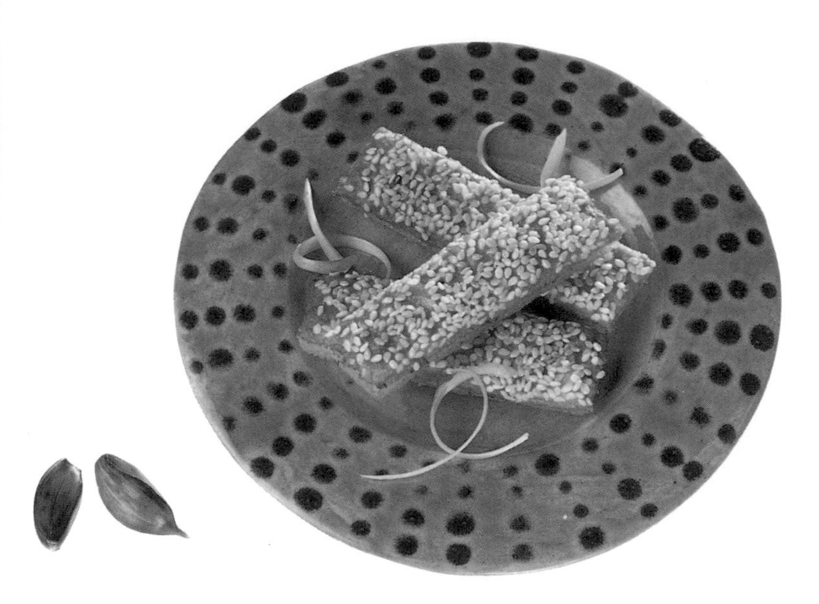

SESAME CHICKEN TOASTS

2 large spring onions
2 cloves garlic, crushed
2.5 cm (1 in) piece fresh root ginger, finely chopped
225 g (8 oz) skinned and boned chicken
2 tablespoons cornflour
2 teaspoons light soy sauce
2 teaspoons oyster sauce
10 slices day-old white bread
55 g (2 oz/⅓ cup) sesame seeds
vegetable oil for frying

In a blender or food processor, process the onions, garlic, ginger, chicken, cornflour and the soy and oyster sauces until smooth.

Cut the crusts off the bread and spread each slice with a generous layer of chicken mixture. Sprinkle with a layer of sesame seeds and place in the refrigerator for at least 20 minutes.

Half-fill a deep fat pan or fryer with oil and heat to 190C (375F) or until a cube of day-old bread browns in 40 seconds. Cut each slice of bread into 3 and fry, a few at a time, until golden. Drain on absorbent kitchen paper and serve hot.

Makes 30.

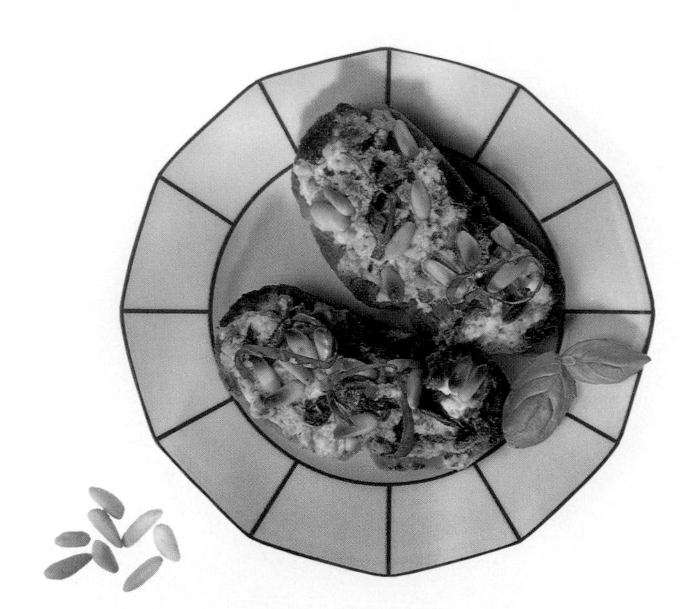

ITALIAN LIVER TOASTS

4 tablespoons oil from a jar of sun-dried tomatoes
1 clove garlic, crushed
1-2 small ciabatta or other Italian bread
115 g (4 oz) chicken livers, cores removed and livers sliced
3 tablespoons ready-made red pesto sauce
115 g (4 oz) ricotta cheese
4 teaspoons shredded basil leaves
4 teaspoons pine nuts

Place the tomato oil and garlic in a bowl and set aside to infuse for 2-3 hours.

Preheat grill. Slice the ciabatta or other bread into 1 cm (½ in) thick slices and brush with the oil. Toast under the hot grill until golden. Heat remaining oil and garlic in a frying pan and quickly fry the livers until lightly browned, then stir in the pesto and remove from the heat.

In a bowl, break up the ricotta and fold in the pesto mixture. Pile each slice of toast with the ricotta mixture, sprinkle with a few basil shreds and some pine nuts and return to the grill for a further 1 minute until bubbly. Serve at once, garnished with basil leaves.

Makes about 20 slices, depending on the size of the bread.

WALDORF SALAD

4 tablespoons mayonnaise
2 tablespoons crème fraîche
1 tablespoons honey
a few drops of lemon juice
salt and pepper
2 teaspoons chopped fresh chives
450 g (1 lb) cooked chicken
175 g (6 oz) seedless muscat grapes
2 eating apples
2 sticks celery
175 g (6 oz/1¾ cups) walnut halves
mixed salad leaves
FOR THE VINAIGRETTE:
4 tablespoons olive oil
1 tablespoon lemon juice

In a bowl, mix together the mayonnaise, crème fraîche and honey. Add the lemon juice, season with salt and pepper and stir in the chopped chives. Remove the skin from the cooked chicken and cut into thin strips. Halve the grapes; core and slice the apples and chop the celery. Add these ingredients to the mayonnaise with the walnuts, then mix gently.

Make the vinaigrette. In a jug, whisk together the oil, lemon juice and salt and pepper; pour over the salad leaves and toss until coated in the dressing. Arrange the salad leaves on a plate and spoon over the chicken mixture.

Serves 4.

—MARINATED CHICKEN SALAD—

150 ml (5 fl oz/⅔ cup) olive oil
4 tablespoons balsamic vinegar
2 tablespoons chopped fresh basil
2 tablespoons chopped fresh rosemary
2 cloves garlic, crushed
4 skinned and boned chicken breasts
1 red pepper (capsicum), deseeded and quartered
1 yellow pepper (capsicum), deseeded and quartered
2 courgettes (zucchini), cut into 1 cm (½ in) thick slices
2 large open cup mushrooms
55 g (2 oz/¼ cup) toasted pine nuts
8 sun-dried tomatoes
½ teaspoon sugar
salt and pepper

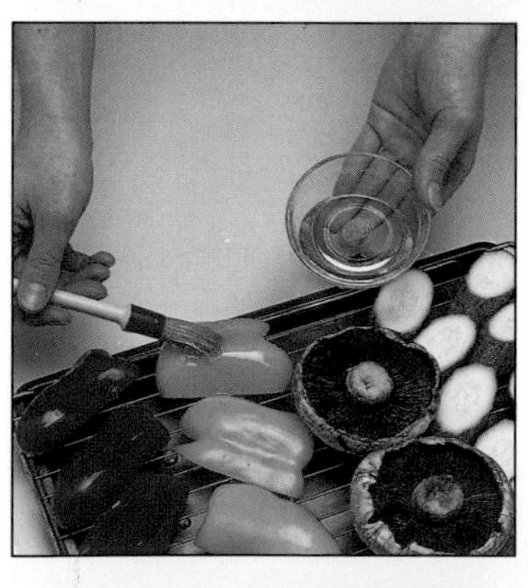

Mix together 4 tablespoons olive oil, 2 tablespoons vinegar, 1 tablespoon basil, 1 tablespoon rosemary and the garlic. Put the chicken into a shallow, flameproof dish and pour over the mixture. Leave for 30 minutes. Preheat grill. Place dish of chicken under the hot grill and cook for 10-14 minutes, turning halfway through cooking until the chicken is brown and crispy; cool. Lay the peppers (capsicums), courgettes (zucchini) and mushrooms in the grill pan, brush with 2 tablespoons oil and grill for about 10 minutes, turning them once: cool.

Peel the skins from the peppers, using a sharp knife, and cut the mushrooms into quarters. Slice the chicken breasts into 2.5 cm (1 in) thick slices and arrange with the grilled vegetables in a dish. Sprinkle over the pine nuts and sun-dried tomatoes. In a small jug, mix the remaining herbs with the oil and vinegar. Add the sugar and season with a little salt and pepper. Pour over the chicken and marinate for 1 hour, stirring occasionally.

Serves 4.

—TROPICAL CHICKEN SALAD—

2 cooked smoked chicken breasts, weighing about 150 g (5 oz) each
2 ripe avocados
2 large ripe mangoes
1 head each of red and white chicory, trimmed
55 g (2 oz) rocket, cleaned
8 teaspoons bottled dill sauce
1 teaspoon crushed pink peppercorns
2 teaspoons white wine vinegar
2 tablespoons olive oil

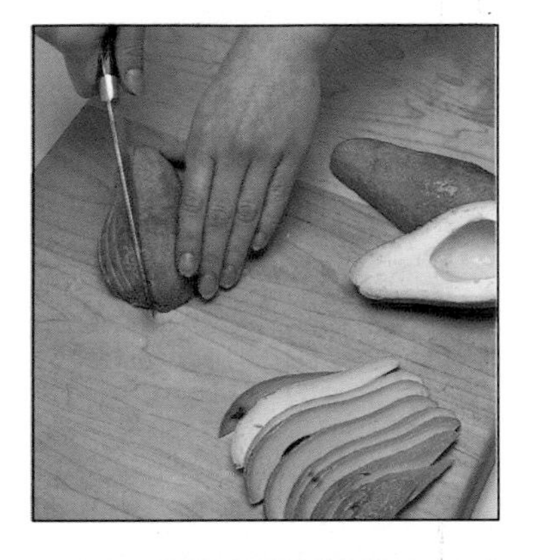

Cut the chicken crossways into thin slices. Remove the skin and stone from the avocados and cut each half lengthways into slices.

Cut each mango in half by cutting either side of the fibrous stone, peel and thinly slice. Separate the chicory into leaves and arrange with the rocket on 4 plates. Place alternate slices of avocado and mango on top of the leaves and arrange a quarter of the chicken slices on each serving.

Whisk together the dill sauce, peppercorns, vinegar and oil and drizzle over each salad. Serve with warm poppy seed rolls.

Serves 4.

CHICKEN SATAY SALAD

2 tablespoons dry sherry
4 tablespoons crunchy peanut butter
2.5 cm (1 in) piece fresh root ginger, finely chopped
2 tablespoons hoisin sauce
3 teaspoons lemon juice
2 tablespoons dark soy sauce
150 ml (5 fl oz/⅔) cup chicken stock or water
4 tablespoons sunflower seeds
2 teaspoons sesame oil
2 tablespoons vegetable oil
salt and pepper
1 Cos lettuce, washed and broken into leaves
115 g (4 oz) beansprouts
115 g (4 oz) cooked green beans
4 skinned and boned chicken breasts

Mix together the sherry, peanut butter, ginger, hoisin sauce, 2 teaspoons of the lemon juice and 1 tablespoon of the soy sauce. Mix well, then beat in the stock or water. Put the sunflower seeds in a pan over a high heat. Stir constantly and after about 1 minute the seeds should start to turn golden. Still stirring, add the remaining soy sauce; it will instantly evaporate and coat the seeds. Tip the seeds onto a saucer and leave to cool. Mix together the sesame oil, 1 tablespoon vegetable oil, the remaining lemon juice and salt and pepper.

Put the lettuce leaves and beansprouts into a bowl, pour over the salad dressing and toss gently. Arrange the leaves and beans on 4 serving plates. Slice chicken into thin strips. In a frying pan, heat the remaining 1 tablespoon vegetable oil and add the chicken. Stir-fry over a high heat until the chicken starts to brown. Lower the heat and pour over the peanut butter mixture; stir until the sauce is simmering and thick. Spoon over the salad leaves and sprinkle with the sunflower seeds.

Serves 4.

YELLOW SALAD

1 clove garlic, crushed
2 teaspoons wholegrain mustard
1 teaspoon clear honey
3 tablespoons white wine vinegar
8 tablespoons olive oil
2 tablespoons chopped fresh chives, plus extra to serve
150 ml (5 fl oz/⅔ cup) natural yogurt
a large pinch of saffron strands
850 ml (30 fl oz/3¾ cups) chicken stock
2 skinned and boned chicken breasts
175 g (6 oz/1¼ cups) pasta shapes
3 yellow peppers (capsicums), halved and deseeded
55 g (2 oz) sun-dried tomatoes
6 spring onions
1 celery heart, with leaves
salt and pepper

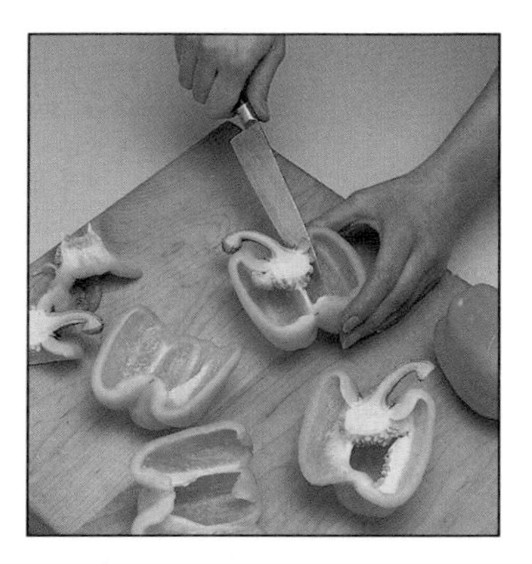

In a bowl, whisk together the garlic, mustard, honey, vinegar, oil, chives and yogurt and reserve. Soak the saffron strands in the chicken stock in a pan, bring to the boil, then reduce to a simmer. Add the chicken breasts and poach gently for 15 minutes. Drain and set aside to cool slightly. Add the pasta to the poaching liquor and cook for 8-10 minutes until the pasta is *al dente* (cooked but firm to the bite). Drain well and pour over the reserved dressing. Preheat grill.

Place the peppers cut-sides down under the hot grill until the skins blacken and blister. Remove and allow to cool, then peel off the blackened skins, cut into thick strips and stir into the pasta. Cut the chicken into strips, slice the tomatoes, spring onions and celery heart and stir into the pasta. Season to taste with salt and plenty of ground black pepper, sprinkle with remaining chives and serve warm or cold with chunks of garlic bread.

Serves 4.

– WARM CHICKEN LIVER SALAD –

175 g (6 oz) young spinach leaves, cleaned
1 small radicchio, cleaned
2 oranges, peeled and cut into segments
1 red onion, sliced into rings
25 g (1 oz/6 teaspoons) butter
3 teaspoons hazelnut oil
450 g (1 lb) chicken livers, cores removed and livers halved
1 clove garlic, crushed
1 tablespoon sherry vinegar
1 heaped teaspoon wholegrain mustard
3 tablespoons dry sherry
1 teaspoon clear honey
salt and pepper
15 g (½ oz/3 teaspoons) roughly chopped toasted hazelnuts, to garnish

Arrange the spinach and radicchio leaves on 4 plates and scatter over the orange segments and onion rings.

In a heavy-based frying pan, heat the butter and oil, add the chicken livers and cook, stirring, over a high heat until well browned. Push the livers to the side of the pan, then add the garlic, vinegar, mustard, sherry, honey and seasonings, bring to the boil and reduce slightly. Add the livers to the sauce and coat well, then spoon onto the salad. Sprinkle with the chopped toasted hazelnuts.

Serves 4.

SPICY THAI SALAD

2 teaspoons sesame oil
2 red chillies, deseeded and chopped
1 clove garlic, crushed
juice of 1 lime
2 teaspoons brown sugar
1 tablespoon fish sauce
1 stem lemon grass, chopped
2 tablespoons shredded fresh basil
225 g (8 oz) cooked chicken, shredded
55 g (2 oz) rice noodles
4 spring onions, sliced into matchstick strips
1 large carrot, cut into matchstick strips
1 yellow pepper (capsicum), cut into matchstick strips
3 Chinese leaves, shredded
2 tablespoons dry roasted peanuts, chopped

In a small pan, heat the oil and quickly fry the chillies and garlic, then remove from the heat and stir in the lime juice, sugar, fish sauce, lemon grass and basil. Pour mixture over the shredded chicken and allow to stand for 30 minutes.

Cook the rice noodles according to the packet instructions, then drain, rinse well in cold water and drain well again. Mix together the noodles, onions, carrot, pepper (capsicum) and Chinese leaves. Spoon over the chicken and sauce and sprinkle with the chopped peanuts.

Serves 4.

CORONATION CHICKEN

1 tablespoon olive oil
1 small onion, diced
2 teaspoons mild curry paste
200 g (7 oz) can chopped tomatoes
55 ml (2 fl oz/¼ cup) white wine
2 tablespoons hot mango chutney, chopped if necessary
2 teaspoons apricot jam
2 teaspoons lemon juice
150 ml (5 fl oz/⅔ cup) mayonnaise
150 ml (5 fl oz/⅔ cup) Greek yogurt
450 g (1 lb) cooked chicken
350 g (12 oz/2 cups) cooked, long-grain rice
1 red pepper (capsicum), diced
2 tablespoons chopped fresh mint
3 tablespoons prepared vinaigrette

In a small saucepan, heat the oil and fry the onion gently without browning until the onion is soft. Stir in the curry paste, tomatoes and wine, bring to the boil and simmer gently for 15 minutes. Add the chutney, jam and lemon juice and cook for a further 5 minutes until thick and syrupy.

Remove from the heat and strain into a small bowl; set aside to cool. When completely cold, stir in the mayonnaise and yogurt and mix well. Cut the chicken into large pieces and stir into the sauce. Combine the rice, pepper (capsicum), mint and vinaigrette and spoon onto a large serving dish and pile the chicken in the centre.

Serves 4.

MEXICAN CHICKEN SALAD

115 g (4 oz/⅔ cup) canned kidney beans, drained
115 g (4 oz/⅔ cup) canned chick peas, drained
1 red pepper (capsicum), sliced
3 Little Gem lettuces, shredded
3 teaspoons made English mustard
2 teaspoons sugar
2 tablespoons red wine vinegar
150 ml (5 fl oz/⅔ cup) olive oil
salt and pepper
4 teaspoons paprika
2 teaspoons cayenne pepper
1 teaspoon chilli powder
4 skinned and boned chicken breasts, cut into strips
2 tablespoons vegetable oil

Mix together the kidney beans, chick peas, red pepper (capsicum) and shredded lettuce and arrange on 4 serving plates. In a bowl, whisk together the mustard, sugar and vinegar and slowly drizzle in the olive oil, whisking well all the time to make a dressing the consistency of runny mayonnaise. Season with salt and pepper and set aside.

Mix the paprika, cayenne pepper and chilli powder together on a plate. Add the strips of chicken and toss until evenly coated in the mixture. Heat the vegetable oil in a frying pan and fry the coated chicken for 2-3 minutes or until cooked. Spoon the chicken over the salad and pour over the salad dressing. Serve immediately.

Serves 4.

CLUBHOUSE SALAD

2 thick slices white bread, crusts removed
oil for frying
350 g (12 oz) cooked chicken breasts
175 g (6 oz) cooked smoked ham
175 g (6 oz) Emmental cheese
1 ripe avocado
2 hard-boiled eggs, shelled
5 tablespoons mayonnaise
1 tablespoon chopped fresh parsley
4 tablespoons olive oil
1 tablespoon white wine vinegar
salt and pepper
1 teaspoon Dijon mustard
1 teaspoon granulated sugar
mixed salad leaves, washed and trimmed
16 cherry tomatoes, halved

Cut the bread into small cubes. Heat 5 cm (2 in) oil in a pan and fry the cubes of bread until golden brown. Remove with a slotted spoon and leave to drain on absorbent kitchen paper. Slice the chicken into strips; cut the ham into 2.5 cm (1 in) cubes; cut the Emmental into strips. Peel and core the avocado and cut into cubes. Cut each egg into quarters. Mix together the mayonnaise and chopped parsley, add the chicken, ham, Emmental, hard-boiled eggs and avocado and mix gently until all the ingredients are well coated in mayonnaise.

In a jug, whisk together the oil, vinegar, salt and pepper, mustard and sugar. Put the salad leaves, cherry tomatoes and croûtons in a bowl, pour over the dressing and toss the salad. Arrange the salad on a plate and spoon over the chicken and ham mixture.

Serves 4.

—CHICKEN & SAFFRON SAUCE—

45 g (1½ oz) fresh root ginger, peeled and chopped
1 clove garlic, crushed
2 teaspoons each ground cumin and coriander
4 cardamom pods, cracked and the seeds crushed
finely grated rind and juice of ½ lemon
½ teaspoon garam masala
150 ml (5 fl oz/⅔ cup) Greek yogurt
4 boned and skinned chicken breasts
pinch of saffron strands
1 tablespoon hot water
1 shallot, finely chopped
55 ml (2 fl oz/¼ cup) dry white wine
150 ml (5 fl oz/⅔ cup) chicken stock
85 ml (3 fl oz/⅓ cup) double (thick) cream
1 tablespoon chopped fresh coriander

In a blender or food processor, purée the ginger with the garlic, cumin, coriander, crushed cardamom seeds, lemon rind and garam masala. Add two-thirds of the yogurt, mix well and put to one side. Cut each chicken breast into 8 strips, put into shallow dish and spoon over the yogurt mixture. Cover and marinate for 1½-2 hours. Meanwhile, soak the saffron strands in the hot water. Put the shallot in a small pan with the wine and boil rapidly until reduced by half. Add the stock, saffron and water and boil until reduced to about 150 ml (5 fl oz/⅔ cup).

Add the cream and simmer for about 2 minutes until the sauce starts to thicken. Leave to cool, then add the remaining yogurt and season with a little lemon juice, salt and pepper. Remove the chicken strips from the marinade and place on a grill pan, leaving a slight gap between the strips to ensure even cooking. Grill for 5 minutes until browned, turning halfway through cooking. Arrange on a serving dish and cool. Drizzle over the sauce and sprinkle with the chopped coriander.

Serves 4.

- CHICKEN & HAM CROQUETTES -

55 g (2 oz/¼ cup) butter
1 onion, finely chopped
55 g (2 oz/½ cup) plain flour
300 ml (10 fl oz/1¼ cups) milk
300 g (10 oz) cooked chicken, finely chopped
55 g (2 oz) ham, finely chopped
2 tablespoons chopped fresh parsley
1 teaspoon Dijon mustard
salt and pepper
85 g (3 oz/1½ cups) fresh white breadcrumbs
vegetable oil for frying
lemon wedges and green salad, to serve

Melt the butter, add the onion and fry gently for 3-4 minutes until soft but not browned.

Add the flour and cook for 1 minute. Gradually blend in the milk and bring to the boil, stirring all the time. Reduce heat and simmer for 2 minutes until sauce forms a thick paste. Add the chopped chicken, ham, parsley, mustard and season with a little salt and pepper. Mix well and put to one side to cool. Place the breadcrumbs on a board and drop tablespoonsful of the mixture onto the breadcrumbs.

Roll mixture in crumbs to give an even coating. Chill for 30 minutes. Heat 5 cm (2 in) oil in a frying pan. Fry the croquettes until golden brown all over. Drain on kitchen paper. Serve with wedges of lemon and a salad.

Makes 12-14.

Note: To make a sauce to serve with the croquettes, mix 2 teaspoons chopped capers with 3 tablespoons crème fraîche and a squeeze of lemon.

-HONEY CHICKEN DRUMSTICKS-

8 chicken drumsticks
4 tablespoons clear honey
2 teaspoons Dijon mustard
2 teaspoons wholegrain mustard
1 teaspoon soy sauce
1 teaspoon dried rosemary

Cut 3 diagonal slashes in the flesh on both sides of the drumsticks and place in a shallow, ovenproof dish or roasting tin.

Mix together the honey, mustards and soy sauce and pour over the drumsticks. Cover and leave to marinate for 1 hour, turning from time to time.

Preheat the oven to 200C (400F/Gas 6). Sprinkle the rosemary over the drumsticks and cook on the top shelf of the oven for 25 minutes. Increase the heat to 230C (450F/Gas 8) and cook for a further 10 minutes, basting and turning the drumsticks several times. Any leftover marinade from the pan can be added to 4 tablespoons mayonnaise with a squeeze of lemon to serve with the drumsticks.

Serves 4.

— DOLCELATTE & PEAR GRILLS —

4 muffins
55 g (2 oz/¼ cup) garlic and herb-flavoured butter
2 small cooked chicken breasts
85 g (3 oz/⅔ cup) dolcelatte cheese
1 small dessert pear, cored and sliced
freshly ground black pepper
watercress sprigs, to garnish

Preheat grill. Split the muffins in half and toast on both sides until lightly browned.

Spread with a little flavoured butter. Cut the chicken and cheese into thin slices. Arrange alternate pieces of chicken, cheese and pear on top of each muffin half.

Sprinkle with black pepper and return to the grill until the cheese has melted. Serve at once, garnished with sprigs of watercress.

Serves 4.

—CHICKEN & SCRAMBLED EGG—

115 g (4 oz) cooked smoked chicken
55 g (2 oz/¼ cup) butter
6 large eggs
2 tablespoons double (thick) cream
juice of ½ lemon
salt and pepper
4 thick slices of brioche
1-2 tablespoons chopped fresh chives

Cut the chicken into matchstick strips. In a non-stick pan, melt the butter, add the chicken strips and cook for 1 minute.

Whisk the eggs with 1 tablespoon of the cream and half of the lemon juice. Season well with black pepper and pour onto the chicken. Cook over a very low heat, stirring continuously, until the egg thickens. Remove from the heat when eggs are almost fully cooked, but still creamy, stir in the remaining cream and lemon juice and season to taste.

Toast the brioche, and put onto 4 warmed serving plates. Top with generous spoonfuls of the scrambed egg mixture and sprinkle with chives and freshly ground black pepper.

Serves 4.

CHICKEN & HAM CRÊPES

1 small onion, quartered
550 ml (20 fl oz/2½ cups) milk
1 bay leaf
25 g (1 oz/6 teaspoons) butter
25 g (1 oz/¼ cup) plain flour
85 g (3 oz/¾ cup) grated mature Cheddar
225 g (8 oz) cooked chicken, diced
225 g (8 oz) broccoli flowerets, cooked al dente
8 thin slices ham
FOR THE PANCAKES:
115 g (4 oz/1 cup) plain flour
1 egg
225 ml (8 fl oz/1 cup) milk
55 ml (2 fl oz/¼ cup) beer
salt and pepper
oil for frying

Put the onion, milk and bay leaf into a small saucepan, bring to the boil and simmer gently for 10-15 minutes until the onion softens. Discard the bay leaf and purée the onion and milk in a blender or food processor. Melt the butter in a pan, stir in the flour and cook for 1 minute, then add the onion milk a little at a time, stirring well between each addition, and bring to the boil.

Remove from the heat, pour half the sauce into a bowl and stir in 55 g (2 oz/½ cup) of the cheese. Add the chicken and broccoli to the remaining sauce in the pan and return to the heat to warm through.

Meanwhile, make the pancakes. In a blender or food processor, blend together all the pancake ingredients, except the oil, to form a creamy batter. Heat a 15 cm (6 in) pancake pan, brush with a very little oil and pour in about 2-3 tablespoons of pancake batter, tilting the pan to cover the base of the pan with a thin layer. Cook until the top is opaque, then flip over and cook the other side. Place between 2 plates over a pan of simmering water to keep warm, while cooking the remaining batter in the same way to make 8 in total.

Preheat grill. Lay a slice of ham on each pancake and top with generous spoonful of chicken mixture. Roll each pancake to enclose the filling and place, fold-side down, in a buttered flameproof dish.

Spoon over the reserved cheese sauce and sprinkle the remaining cheese on top. Place under the hot grill until golden and bubbly.

Serves 4.

HERBY CHICKEN FRITTATA

2 tablespoons olive oil
2 large onions, thinly sliced
175 g (6 oz) waxy potatoes
5 large eggs
85 g (3 oz/¾ cup) grated mature Cheddar cheese
2 tablespoons finely chopped parsley
salt and pepper
25 g (1 oz/6 teaspoons) butter
175 g (6 oz) cooked chicken, cut into chunks
parsley sprigs, to garnish

Heat the oil and fry the onions for 20 minutes until golden brown; allow to cool slightly. Cook the potatoes in boiling, salted water until just tender. Cut into bite-sized chunks.

Beat together the eggs, cooked onions, cheese and parsley and season with salt and pepper. Melt the butter in the frying pan and stir in the chicken, pour in the egg mixture, then stir in the potatoes and allow to cook over a very gentle heat until the base sets and the top is runny. Preheat grill.

Cook the frittata top under the hot grill until it is golden and bubbly. Serve at once, cut into wedges and garnished with sprigs of parsley.

Serves 4.

ORIENTAL FRIED RICE

175 g (6 oz/1 ¼ cups) long-grain rice
300 ml (10 fl oz/1 ¼ cups) chicken stock
2 tablespoons sesame oil
1 cm (½ in) cube fresh root ginger, grated
1 clove garlic, crushed
175 g (6 oz) raw chicken, thinly sliced
6 spring onions, sliced
1 small red pepper (capsicum), deseeded and sliced
115 g (4 oz) cooked peeled prawns
2 large eggs
2 tablespoons light soy sauce
1 tablespoon chopped fresh coriander
55 g (2 oz/⅓ cup) toasted cashew nuts

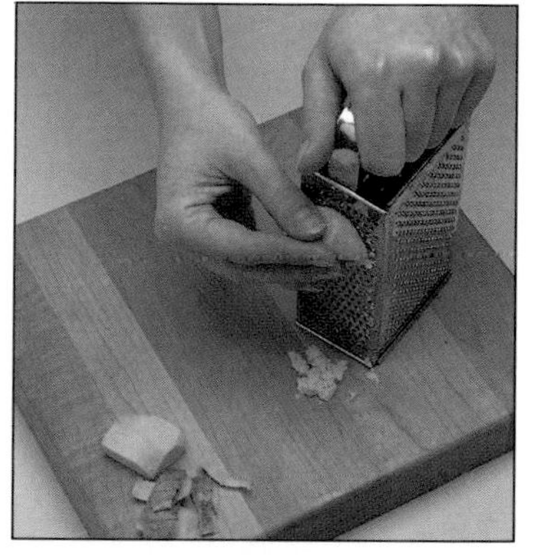

Put the rice and stock into a pan, bring to the boil, cover and simmer gently for 10 minutes. Remove from the heat and leave for a further 10 minutes. Drain off any excess liquid and allow to cool slightly. Heat the sesame oil in a large frying pan or wok and add the ginger, garlic and chicken and stir-fry for 4-5 minutes until the chicken is cooked.

Add the onions, pepper (capsicum) and prawns and stir-fry for a further 1 minute. In a bowl, beat together the eggs and the soy sauce and stir in the rice. Tip onto the chicken mixture and continue to cook over a high heat for 1 minute, stirring. Remove from the heat and stir in the coriander. Serve garnished with toasted cashew nuts.

Serves 4.

CHICKEN STIR-FRY

350 g (12 oz) skinned and boned chicken breasts
2 tablespoons soy sauce
3 tablespoons dry sherry
3 tablespoons vegetable oil
1 clove garlic, finely chopped
2.5 cm (1 in) piece fresh root ginger, chopped
1 small red pepper (capsicum), deseeded and sliced
4 spring onions, cut into 2.5 cm (1 in) lengths
55 g (2 oz) mange tout (snow peas), topped and tailed
8 baby corn, cut into halves lengthways
1 teaspoon cornflour
few drops sesame oil
few drops lemon juice

Cut the chicken breast into thin strips. Place in a bowl and add 1 teaspoon soy sauce and 1 tablespoon sherry and leave to marinate for 35 minutes. In a wok or large frying pan, heat the oil over a high heat, add the garlic and ginger and stir-fry for 15 seconds, then add the chicken and stir-fry for 2-3 minutes. Add the red pepper (capsicum), spring onions, mange tout (snow-peas) and baby corn and stir-fry for a further 1 minute.

Mix together the cornflour with the remaining soy sauce and sherry, pour the mixture into the wok and cook for 30 seconds until the sauce thickens and glazes the ingredients. Just before serving drizzle over the sesame oil and the lemon juice.

Serves 4.

COQ AU VIN

550 ml (20 fl oz/2 ½ cups) red wine
3 cloves garlic, sliced
1 small onion, chopped
2 tablespoons olive oil
1 teaspoon brown sugar
1 teaspoon mixed peppercorns, crushed
1 teaspoon coriander seeds, crushed
1 bouquet garni
1.5 kg (3 ¼-3 ½ lb) chicken, cut into 8 pieces
45 g (1 ½ oz/3 tablespoons) seasoned flour
115 g (4 oz) piece smoked bacon, derinded and diced
175 g (6 oz) button onions, peeled
175 g (6 oz) button mushrooms
425 ml (15 fl oz/2 cups) chicken stock
2 tablespoons chopped parsley
fried bread croûtons, to garnish

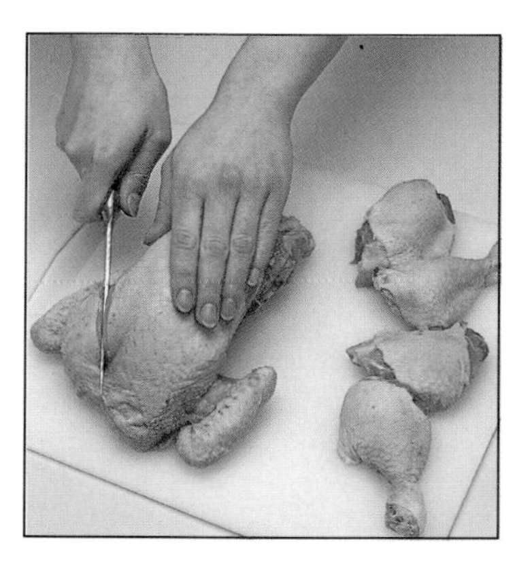

Mix together the wine, garlic, chopped onion, 1 tablespoon of the oil, sugar, peppercorns and coriander. Add the bouquet garni and the chicken pieces. Cover and marinate in the refrigerator for 2-3 hours, turning regularly. Remove chicken from marinade (reserving marinade) and pat dry on kitchen paper, then toss in the seasoned flour. Heat the remaining oil in a casserole and fry the bacon until browned, remove with a slotted spoon and set to one side. Add the chicken pieces to the casserole and fry until well browned, set aside with the bacon.

Add the button onions and cook until browned. Add mushrooms and any remaining flour. Cook for 1 minute. Add the stock and marinade, stirring until thick. Return chicken and bacon, cover and simmer for 40 minutes. Remove the chicken and vegetables to a serving dish using a slotted spoon; keep warm. Bring the sauce to the boil for 3-4 minutes until thick. Check the seasoning and stir in the parsley. Spoon the sauce over the chicken and garnish with bread croûtons.

Serves 4.

-CHICKEN VEGETABLE HOTPOT-

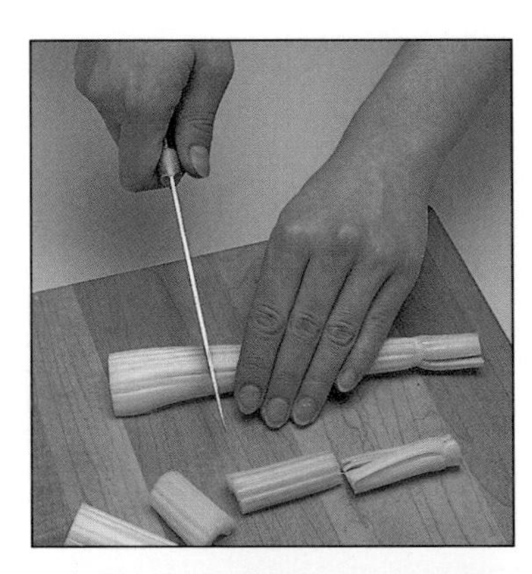

55 g (2 oz/¼ cup) butter
115 g (4 oz) smoked bacon, chopped
2 large chicken quarters, halved
2 carrots, peeled and sliced
1 onion, sliced
2 sticks celery, cut into 5 cm (2 in) lengths
2 leeks, trimmed and sliced
2 tablespoons plain flour
1 kg (2 lb) potatoes, peeled
2 tablespoons chopped fresh thyme
2 tablespoons chopped fresh parsley
salt and pepper
425 ml (15 fl oz/2 cups) chicken stock

Preheat oven to 150C (300F/Gas 2). Heat half the butter in a frying pan, add the bacon and chicken and fry until golden. Remove from the pan and drain on absorbent kitchen paper to remove excess fat. Add the carrots, onion, celery and leeks to the pan and fry for 2-3 minutes until the vegetables are turning golden. Sprinkle over the flour and mix well.

Slice the potatoes into 0.5 cm (¼ in) thick slices. Arrange half the slices in the bottom of a casserole, add the chicken and bacon, cover with the vegetables and chopped herbs and season well with salt and pepper. Cover with the remaining sliced potato, dot with the remaining butter and pour over the stock. Cover and bake for 1 hour, then uncover and continue cooking for a further 25-30 minutes until the chicken is tender and cooked and the potatoes are crisp and brown.

Serves 4.

CHICKEN IN CAPER SAUCE

1 onion, quartered
1 carrot, peeled and quartered
1 teaspoon finely grated orange rind
1 orange, peeled and sliced
bay leaves
55 ml (2 oz/¼ cup) dry white wine
225 ml (8 fl oz/1 cup) chicken stock
4 skinned and boned chicken breasts
25 g (1 oz/6 teaspoons) butter
25 g (1 oz/¼ cup) plain flour
150 ml (5 fl oz/⅔ cup) single (light) cream
1 tablespoon chopped fresh parsley
2 teaspoons capers, drained

Place the first 5 ingredients in a frying pan.

Add the wine and stock and bring to the boil. Add the chicken breasts, reduce the heat until barely simmering, then cover and poach for 20 minutes or until cooked. Remove the cooked breasts, drain well on absorbent kitchen paper and keep warm. Strain and reserve the poaching liquor.

In a pan, melt the butter, add the flour and cook for 1 minutes, remove from the heat and slowly add the poaching liquor, stirring well between each addition. Return to the heat and bring to the boil, stirring continuously, until thickened. Stir in the cream, parsley and capers and season to taste. Spoon over the chicken breasts and serve with cardamom-scented rice.

Serves 4.

LEMON CHICKEN

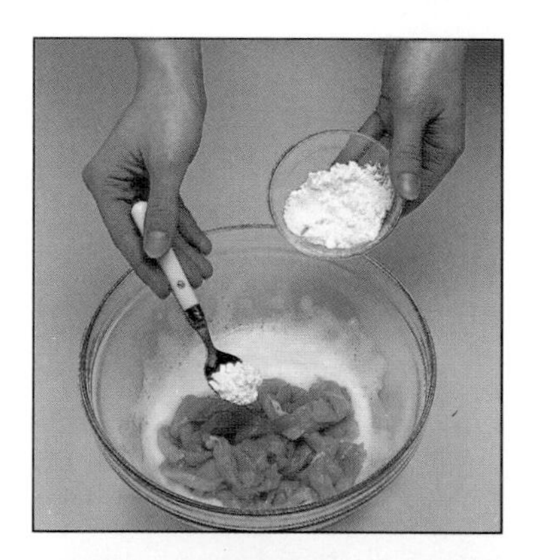

1 egg white
350 g (12 oz) chicken breast, sliced
3 teaspoons cornflour
finely grated rind and juice of 1 lemon
2 tablespoons dry sherry
1 teaspoon soy sauce
2 teaspoon clear honey
3 tablespoons vegetable oil
4 spring onions, sliced
55 g (2 oz) mange tout (snow peas), topped and tailed
½ red pepper (capsicum), finely sliced
55 g (2 oz) beansprouts

Whisk egg white until frothy. Stir in chicken, 2 teaspoons cornflour and lemon rind.

In another bowl, mix together the remaining cornflour, sherry, lemon juice, soy sauce and honey. Put to one side. Heat the oil in a wok or large frying pan, add the chicken pieces a few at a time to prevent them sticking together. Stir-fry for 2 minutes or until the chicken is cooked through.

Add the spring onions, mange tout (snow peas), red pepper (capsicum) and beansprouts and continue to stir-fry for a further 1 minute. Add the lemon juice and cornflour mixture and cook for 1-2 minutes, stirring until the sauce thickens and coats the chicken and vegetables.

Serves 4.

CHICKEN CORDON BLEU

4 skinned and boned chicken breasts
4 slices smoked ham
115 g (4 oz) Emmental cheese
2 eggs, beaten
175 g (6 oz/3 cups) fresh white breadcrumbs
oil for deep frying

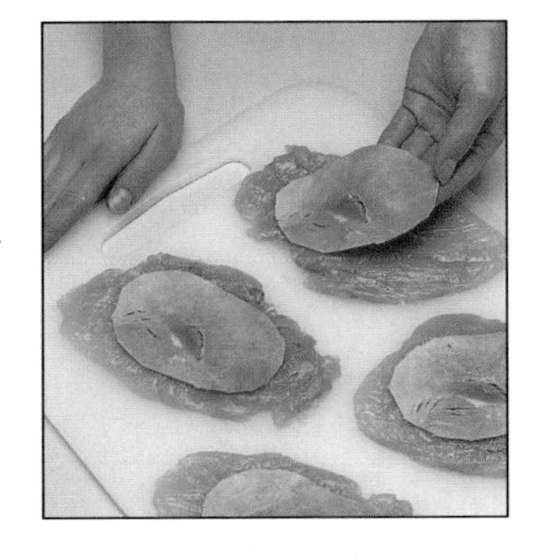

Lay the chicken breasts between 2 sheets of greaseproof paper and beat out with a rolling pin to about 0.5 cm (¼ in) thick, taking care not to tear the flesh. Trim the slices of ham so they are smaller than the chicken breasts and lay a slice on top of each breast.

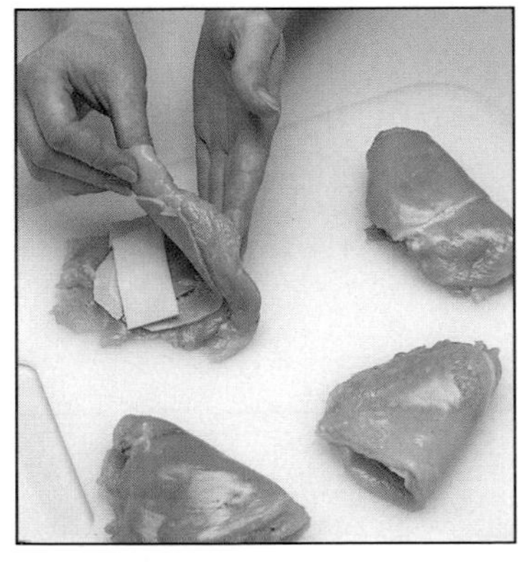

Cut the cheese into very thin slices and place on top of the ham. Fold the chicken breast in half to enclose the filling. Carefully dip each chicken breast first in the beaten egg, then in the breadcrumbs. Repeat this process so that the chicken is well coated and the filling completely enclosed.

Half-fill a deep fat pan or fryer with oil and heat to 190C (375F). Fry the chicken for 7 minutes, then decrease the heat and cook for a further 5 minutes to ensure that the coating doesn't burn before the chicken is cooked. Remove from the oil with a slotted spoon and drain on absorbent kitchen paper. Serve immediately.

Serves 4.

CHICKEN KIEV

115 g (4 oz/½ cup) unsalted butter, softened
3 cloves garlic, crushed
finely grated rind of ½ lemon
1 tablespoon chopped fresh parsley
salt and pepper
4 skinned and boned chicken breasts
2 eggs, beaten
175 g (6 oz/3 cups) fresh white breadcrumbs
oil for deep frying

Beat together the softened butter, crushed garlic, grated lemon rind, parsley and salt and pepper. Transfer to a piping bag fitted with a plain 0.5 cm (¼ in) nozzle.

Lay the chicken breasts on a board and insert a sharp knife into the breast to form a pocket. Take the piping bag and pipe the butter into the pocket (do not over-fill or the butter will burst through the flesh). Leave to refrigerate for 25 minutes.

Dip a filled chicken breast into the beaten eggs, then roll in the breadcrumbs. Repeat once more so chicken is well coated. Repeat with the remaining chicken. Half-fill a deep fat pan or fryer with oil and heat to 190C (375F). Lower in the chicken breasts, 2 at a time, and fry for 8-10 minutes or until cooked through and golden brown. Drain on absorbent kitchen paper and serve immediately with a squeeze of lemon.

Serves 4.

GRILLED CHICKEN & HERBS

4 chicken breasts, on the bone, weighing about 175 g (6 oz) each
2 cloves garlic, peeled and sliced
4 sprigs of fresh rosemary
6 tablespoons olive oil
grated rind and juice of ½ lemon
2 tablespoons dry white wine
salt and pepper
½ teaspoon Dijon mustard
2 tablespoons balsamic vinegar
1 teaspoon sugar

Make several incisions in the chicken breasts and insert pieces of garlic and rosemary. Place the chicken breasts in a flameproof dish.

Mix together 2 tablespoons olive oil with the rind and juice of ½ lemon, the white wine and salt and pepper and pour over the chicken breasts and leave to marinate for 45 minutes. Preheat grill.

Place the chicken breast, skin-sides down, in the dish and cook under the hot grill for 5 minutes. Turn over and spoon the marinade over the top and grill for a further 10 minutes until the skin is crisp and brown. Whisk together the mustard, vinegar, sugar, salt and pepper and remaining oil. Add any cooking juices or marinade from the pan and spoon over the chicken to serve.

Serves 4.

TANDOORI CHICKEN

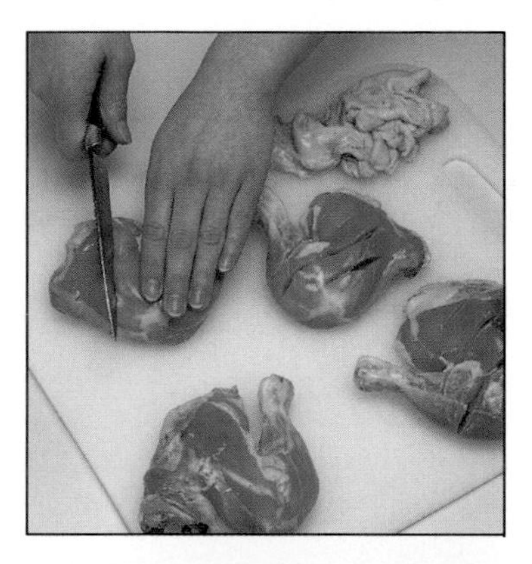

4 chicken leg quarters, skinned
juice of 1 lemon
salt
2 teaspoons ground turmeric
2 teaspoons paprika
1 teaspoon garam masala
1 teaspoon ground cardamom
½ teaspoon chilli powder
pinch saffron powder
2 cloves garlic, crushed
2 teaspoons chopped fresh root ginger
1 tablespoon olive oil
200 ml (7 fl oz/¾ cup) natural yogurt

Cut deep diagonal cuts in the chicken flesh.

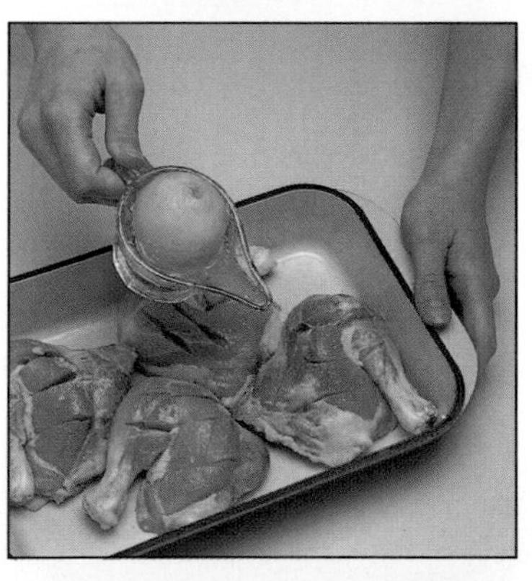

Sprinkle with lemon juice and a little salt. Mix together all the remaining ingredients and use to coat the chicken quarters, cover and leave in a cool place to marinate for 4 hours or overnight.

Preheat grill and cook chicken for 25 minutes, brushing with any excess marinade and turning frequently until the chicken is tender and juices run clear when chicken leg is pierced with a knife. A slight blackening of the chicken gives an authentic look. Serve with wedges of lemon, boiled rice and an onion salad.

Serves 4.

SPATCHCOCK POUSSIN

2 poussins
75 g (3 oz/⅓ cup) butter, softened
4 teaspoons chopped fresh rosemary
4 teaspoons chopped fresh basil
8 sun-dried tomatoes, chopped
finely grated rind and juice of 1 lime
salt and pepper

Prepare the poussins. Using kitchen scissors, cut along the backbone of each poussin. Turn the poussin over so the breast is facing up and flatten the chicken out by pressing down gently on the breast.

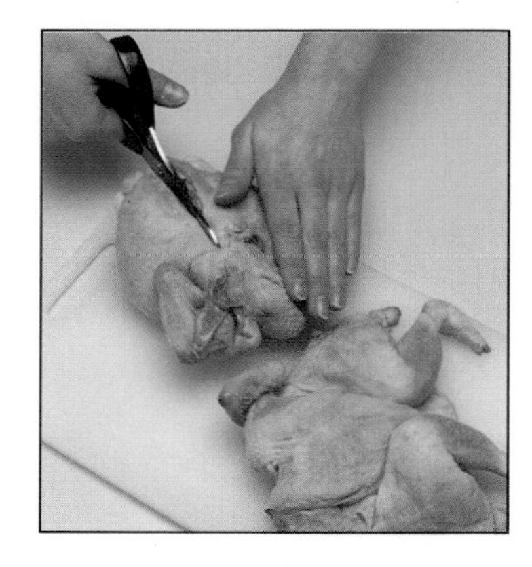

Gently loosen the skin on the breast (starting at the pointed end) by running a sharp knife under the skin, taking care not to tear the skin or cut the flesh. The skin should not be separate but loosened enough to form a pocket in which to put the butter. In a bowl, beat the butter with a fork until soft, add the rosemary, basil, sun-dried tomatoes, rind and juice of the lime, and a little salt and pepper to taste. Preheat grill.

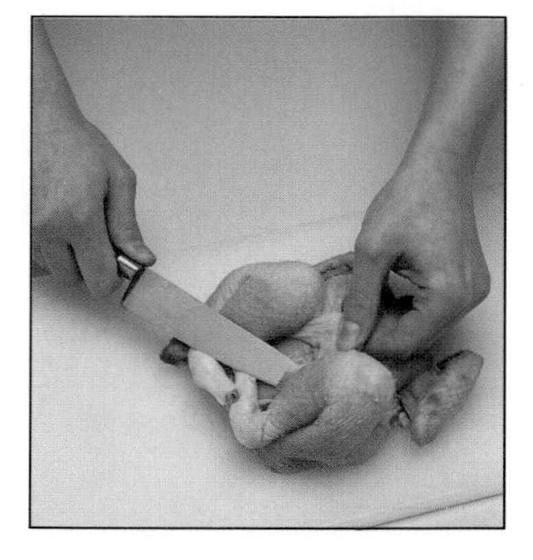

Using a table knife, spread the butter mixture onto the flesh under the skin, making sure the breast is well covered. Place the poussins, breast-sides down, in a grill pan and place under a very hot grill for 10 minutes until brown and crispy. Turn the poussins over and cook for a further 10 minutes until the skins turn crispy, spooning over any melted butter in pan. Serve with boiled new potatoes and a green salad and spoon over any melted butter left in the grill pan.

Serves 2.

HASH RISSOLES

350 g (12 oz) cooked chicken, minced
8 spring onions, chopped
450 g (1 lb) potatoes, boiled and mashed
2 tablespoons mayonnaise
2 tablespoons chopped fresh parsley
½ teaspoon finely grated lemon rind
¼ teaspoon freshly grated nutmeg
salt and pepper
2 large eggs
55 g (2 oz/1 cup) fresh white breadcrumbs
oil for frying

In a bowl, mix together the chicken, onions, potatoes, mayonnaise, parsley, lemon rind, nutmeg, seasonings and one of the eggs.

Form into 8 patties, dip into the remaining beaten egg, then coat in the breadcrumbs and set aside to chill for 20 minutes.

In a large frying pan, heat the oil and cook the patties on both sides for about 5-6 minutes until golden. Drain on absorbent kitchen paper. Serve at once with a crisp green salad and assorted relishes.

Serves 4.

MINTED MEATBALLS

1 small onion, quartered
400 g (14 oz) can chopped tomatoes
300 ml (10 fl oz/1 ¼ cups) chicken stock
grated rind and juice of ½ large orange
2 tablespoons tomato purée (paste)
4 tablespoons chopped fresh mint
1 teaspoon sugar
1 teaspoon red wine vinegar
450 g (1 lb) raw chicken, minced
8 spring onions, finely chopped
55 g (2 oz/1 cup) fresh white breadcrumbs
1 small egg, beaten
2 teaspoons ground cumin
salt and pepper
oil for frying

Place the onion, tomatoes, stock, orange rind and juice, tomato purée (paste), 2 tablespoons chopped mint, sugar and vinegar, in a blender or food processor. Blend until smooth, then pour into a saucepan and simmer for 10-15 minutes. In a large bowl, combine the chicken with the spring onions, breadcrumbs, egg, remaining 2 tablespoons chopped mint, cumin and seasonings. Using wet hands, form the chicken mixture into 40 small balls.

In a large non-stick pan, heat a little oil and fry the meatballs for about 6-8 minutes until slightly coloured all over. Remove from the pan and drain on absorbent kitchen paper. Wipe out the frying pan with absorbent kitchen paper and return the meatballs to the pan, spoon over the sauce and simmer, uncovered, for 15 minutes. Serve on a bed of freshly cooked spaghetti, sprinkle with Parmesan cheese and garnish with mint sprigs.

Serves 4.

PIQUANT MEATLOAF

25 g (1 oz/6 teaspoons) butter
1 onion, finely chopped
1 clove garlic, crushed
85 g (3 oz) mushrooms, coarsely chopped
25 g (1 oz/¼ cup) plain flour
300 ml (10 fl oz/1¼ cups) milk
55 g (2 oz) fresh white breadcrumbs
2 eggs, beaten
finely grated rind and juice of 1 lemon
450 g (1 lb) skinned and boned chicken breasts
55 g (2 oz) streaky bacon, rinds removed
55 g (2 oz) dried apricots, chopped
1 tablespoon chopped fresh thyme
2 tablespoons chopped fresh parsley
¼ teaspoon grated nutmeg
salt and pepper

Preheat the oven to 200C (400F/Gas 6). In a pan, gently melt the butter, add the onion and garlic and fry for 2-3 minutes until softned but not browned. Add the mushrooms and cook for a further 1 minute. Add the flour and cook until all the fat has been absorbed. Remove from the heat and gradually add the milk. Return the pan to the heat and simmer until the sauce has thickened, stirring contantly, then add the breadcrumbs. Transfer to a bowl and allow to cool, then beat in the eggs and lemon juice.

In a food processor, finely process the chicken breast and bacon. Transfer to a bowl and add the apricots, herbs, nutmeg, and lemon rind. Mix well. Add the cooled sauce to the chicken and bacon mixture and mix well. Season with salt and pepper and transfer to a 1 kg (2 lb) loaf tin. Cover the meat loaf with greased foil and put into a roasting pan half-filled with hot water. Bake in the oven for 55-60 minutes or until the loaf is firm to the touch. Serve hot or cold.

Serves 4.

CHICKEN BURGERS

85 g (3 oz) packet country stuffing mix
225 g (8 oz) raw chicken meat, minced
1 small egg, beaten
1 eating apple, peeled, cored and grated
salt and pepper
1-2 tablespoons oil
4 sesame seed baps
iceberg lettuce, shredded
2 tomatoes, sliced
4 squares processed Cheddar cheese slices
mayonnaise and relish, to serve

Make up the stuffing mix according to the packet instructions and set aside to cool.

In a bowl, mix together the chicken, stuffing, egg, apple and seasonings and shape into 4 burgers. In a frying pan, heat the oil and fry the burgers for 6-7 minutes on each side until cooked.

Split the buns in half and cover the bases with the shredded lettuce and tomato slices. Place the burgers over the lettuce and tomato, then cover each burger with a slice of cheese. Spoon on mayonnaise or relish and place the bap top in position.

Serves 4.

FRIED SHREDDED CHICKEN

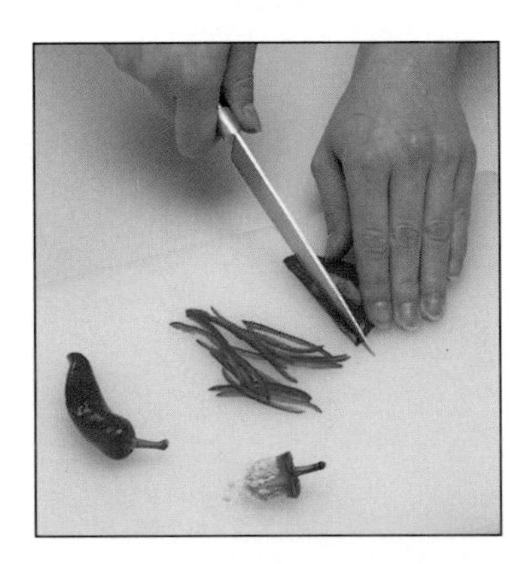

1 egg white
1 tablespoon cornflour
salt and pepper
350 g (12 oz) chicken breast, cut into thin strips
oil for frying
2.5 cm (1 in) cube fresh root ginger, finely chopped
2 cloves garlic, sliced
115 g (4 oz) carrots, cut into matchstick strips
2 teaspoons sesame seeds
2 red chillies, deseeded and thinly sliced
FOR THE SAUCE:
2 teaspoons cornflour
55 ml (2 fl oz/¼ cup) chicken stock
1 teaspoon each chilli sauce, tomato purée (paste) and clear honey
1 tablespoon each dark soy sauce and dry sherry

Beat the egg white with the cornflour. Season the strips of chicken and coat in the egg white mixture. In a deep frying pan or wok, heat the oil and fry the chicken a few strips at a time for 2-3 minutes until golden and crisp. Drain on absorbent kitchen paper while cooking the remainder in the same way. Pour all but 1 tablespoon oil out of the pan. Stir fry the ginger, garlic, carrots, sesame seeds and chillies for 2-3 minutes without colouring.

Blend together all the sauce ingredients and pour onto the vegetables, then bring to the boil and cook, stirring, until thick and glossy. Add the chicken, stir well to coat in the sauce and cook for a further 1-2 minutes. Serve with egg fried rice and garnish with spring onions.

Serves 4.

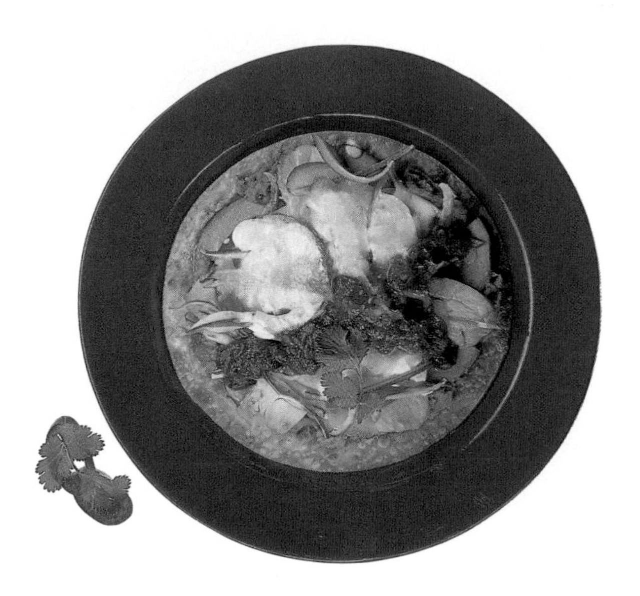

TOSTADAS WITH SALSA

8 corn or wheat fried tortillas
200 g (7 oz) can refried beans
1 avocado, sliced
2 cooked chicken breasts, sliced
115 ml (4 fl oz/½ cup) thick sour cream
4 small tomatoes, sliced
1 red onion, sliced
115 g (4 oz/1 cup) grated Cheddar cheese
FOR THE SALSA:
4 spring onions
200 g (7 oz) can chopped tomatoes
½ teaspoon chilli sauce
1 teaspoon each tomato purée (paste), sugar and red wine vinegar
1 tablespoon chopped fresh coriander
pickled jalapeño peppers, to serve

Preheat grill. Arrange the tortillas on a grill pan. Warm the refried beans and divide equally between the tortillas. Top with the sliced avocado, chicken, thick sour cream, tomatoes and sliced onion and sprinkle with the cheese. Cook under the hot grill until the cheese begins to melt.

In a blender or food processor, blend together all the ingredients for the salsa for 15-20 seconds. Serve with the tortillas and garnish with pickled jalapeño peppers.

Serves 4.

JAMBALAYA

1 tablespoon olive oil
15 g (½ oz/3 teaspoons) butter
350 g (12 oz) skinned and boned chicken meat
175 g (6 oz) chorizo sausage
1 onion, thinly sliced
2 cloves garlic, sliced
1 red pepper (capsicum). sliced
1 yellow pepper (capsicum), sliced
1 green pepper (capsicum), sliced
115 g (4 oz) mushrooms, sliced
150 g (5 oz/1 cup) long-grain rice
½ teaspoon ground allspice
300 ml (10 fl oz/1¼ cups) chicken stock
150 ml (5 fl oz/⅔ cup) white wine
115 g (4 oz) large cooked peeled prawns
lime wedges and whole prawns, to garnish

In a large frying pan or paella pan, heat the oil and butter. Cut the chicken into thick strips and fry until well browned, then remove from the pan and set aside. Cut the chorizo into chunks and fry for 1 minute, stirring well, then using a slotted spoon, remove from the pan and add to the chicken. Fry the onion and garlic until slightly softened, add the peppers (capsicums), mushrooms, rice and allspice and cook for a further 1 minute.

Pour in the stock and wine and bring to the boil, return the chicken and chorizo to the pan and simmer, uncovered, for 15-20 minutes until the liquid is absorbed and the rice tender. Stir in the prawns, cook for a further 5 minutes, then season to taste. Serve garnished with wedges of lime and whole prawns.

Serves 4.

— SOUTHERN-FRIED CHICKEN —

4 chicken breasts
salt and pepper
3 tablespoons paprika
2 tablespoons ground coriander
1 tablespoon ground cumin
finely grated rind and juice of 1 lemon
3 tablespoons dark soy sauce
2 tablespoons chopped fresh coriander
1 teaspoon chopped fresh thyme
1 onion, finely choppd
2 cloves garlic, crushed
1 red chilli pepper, deseeded and chopped
vegetable oil for frying
85 g (3 oz/¾ cup) plain flour
lemon wedges and coriander sprigs, to garnish

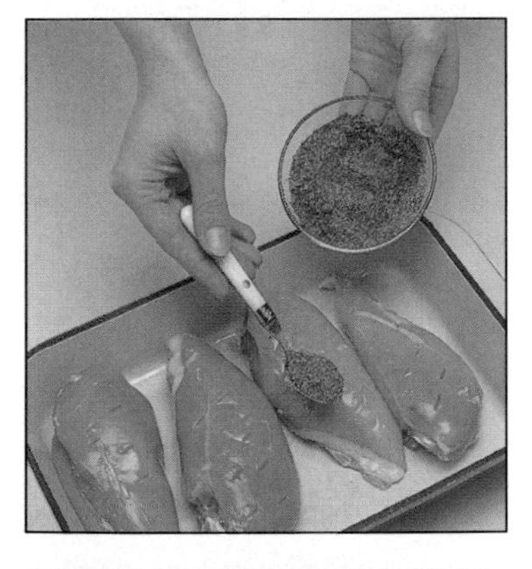

Remove the skin from the chicken breasts. Place the chicken in a shallow dish. Make several incisions in the chicken portions and season well with salt and pepper. In a small bowl, mix together 2 tablespoons paprika, 1 tablespoon ground coriander and 2 teaspoons ground cumin and sprinkle over the chicken. Mix the rind and juice of the lemon with the soy sauce, then add the coriander, thyme, onion, garlic and chilli. Pour over the chicken – making sure it is well covered by the mixture. Cover the dish with cling film and leave to marinate for at least 3 hours or overnight.

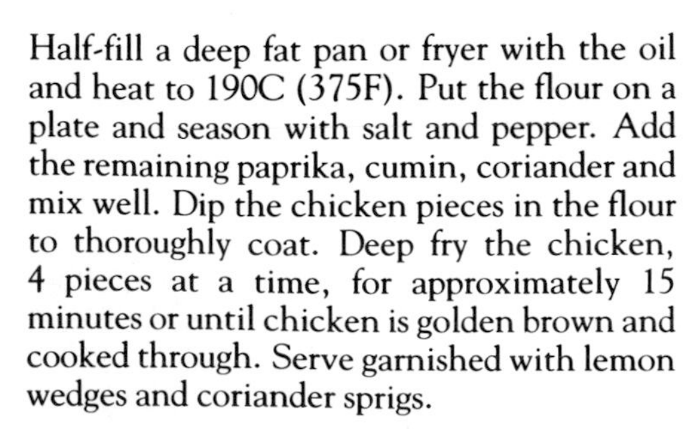

Half-fill a deep fat pan or fryer with the oil and heat to 190C (375F). Put the flour on a plate and season with salt and pepper. Add the remaining paprika, cumin, coriander and mix well. Dip the chicken pieces in the flour to thoroughly coat. Deep fry the chicken, 4 pieces at a time, for approximately 15 minutes or until chicken is golden brown and cooked through. Serve garnished with lemon wedges and coriander sprigs.

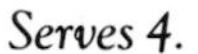

Serves 4.

CHICKEN CHILLI TACOS

2 tablespoons oil
450 g (1 lb) skinned and boned chicken breasts, cubed
8 spring onions, chopped into 2.5 cm (1 in) pieces
1 green pepper (capsicum), chopped
1 clove garlic, crushed
2 fresh green chillies, deseeded and finely chopped
1 teaspoon each fresh basil and oregano
400 g (14 oz) can chopped tomatoes
2 teaspoons chilli sauce
2 teaspoons tomato purée (paste)
1 teaspoon sugar
200 g (7 oz) can red kidney beans, drained
salt and pepper
8 taco shells
1 iceburg lettuce, shredded
150 ml (5 fl oz/$^2/_3$ cup) thick sour cream

In a large frying pan, heat the oil and fry the chicken for 2-3 minutes. Add the spring onions, green pepper (capsicum), garlic, chillies and herbs and cook for a further 2 minutes. Add the chopped tomatoes, chilli sauce, tomato purée (paste), sugar, kidney beans and salt and pepper and simmer for 20-25 minutes or until the sauce starts to thicken.

Spoon some shredded lettuce into each taco shell, top with chilli chicken and spoon over a little thick sour cream.

Serves 4.

Note: Use a mixture of grated cheese, chopped sun-dried tomatoes and chopped olives as a topping for the tacos.

CHICKEN FAJITAS

55 ml (2 fl oz/¼ cup) dry white wine
finely grated rind and juice of 2 limes
1 tablespoon Worcestershire sauce
2 teaspoons brown sugar
½ teaspoon dried basil
½ teaspoon dried oregano
1 clove garlic, crushed
4 skinned and boned chicken breasts
6 teaspoons vegetable oil
8 spring onions, sliced
1 red pepper (capsicum), deseeded and sliced
1 green pepper (capsicum), deseeded and sliced
8 wheat flour tortillas, warmed gently
150 ml (5 fl oz/⅔ cup) thick sour cream
ripe avocado, peeled and chopped

Prepare the marinade for the chicken. In a bowl, mix together the wine, rind and juice of the limes, Worcestershire sauce, sugar, basil, oregano and garlic. Slice the chicken breast into thin strips and add to the marinade. Mix well and leave to marinate for 30-40 minutes, stirring from time to time. In a pan, heat 2 tablespoons oil and add the spring onions and peppers (capsicums) and fry until the onions are starting to colour, but the vegetables are still crisp. Remove from the pan and put to one side. Drain the chicken, reserving the marinade.

Heat the remaining oil, and when very hot, add the chicken and fry quickly until golden brown. Remove from the pan with a slotted spoon; set aside. Add the reserved marinade to the pan and boil until thickened and reduced. Return the chicken and peppers and mix well until all ingredients are coated in the marinade. Put tortillas on a plate, place the chicken mixture in the middle, spoon over some thick sour cream and chopped avocado. Roll up and serve.

Serves 4.

—CHICKEN & CORN FRITTERS—

1 banana
1 egg
85 g (3 oz) cooked chicken, finely chopped
200 g (7 oz) can sweetcorn kernels, drained
2 spring onions, finely chopped
½ teaspoon ground cumin
2 teaspoons chopped fresh coriander
salt and cayenne pepper
85 g (3 oz/¾ cup) self-raising flour
oil for frying

Mash the banana. Mix in the egg, chicken, sweetcorn, spring onions, cumin, coriander, salt and a pinch of cayenne pepper. Add the flour and form a soft batter.

Heat oil in a heavy frying pan or saucepan and add spoonfuls of the mixture, cooking for about 1 minute, turning halfway through cooking, until golden brown.

Remove from the pan with a slotted spoon and drain on absorbent kitchen paper. Serve the fritters warm with a chilli dip or relish.

Serves 4.

GUMBO

25 g (1 oz/6 teaspoons) butter
1 tablespoon oil
1.5 kg (3¼-3½ lb) chicken, cut into 8 pieces
25 g (1 oz/¼ cup) seasoned flour
1 large onion, sliced
2 cloves garlic, sliced
2 teaspoons chilli powder
400 g (14 oz) can chopped tomatoes
2 tablespoons tomato purée (paste)
300 ml (10 fl oz/1¼ cups) chicken stock
115 ml (4 fl oz/½ cup) red wine
1 red pepper (capsicum), deseeded and sliced
1 green pepper (capsicum), deseeded and sliced
350 g (12 oz) small okra, trimmed
2 teaspoons lemon juice
pinch of sugar

Preheat oven to 180C (350F/Gas 4). Heat the butter and oil in a flameproof casserole. Toss the chicken pieces in the seasoned flour, then fry in the hot fats until golden. Remove from the pan and set aside. Cook the onion and garlic in the casserole until slightly softened, stir in the chilli powder and any remaining flour, then add the tomatoes, tomato purée (paste), stock and wine and bring to the boil.

Stir in the vegetables, lemon juice and sugar and return the chicken to the casserole. Cover and cook in the oven for 50-60 minutes. Serve with rice, if wished.

Serves 4.

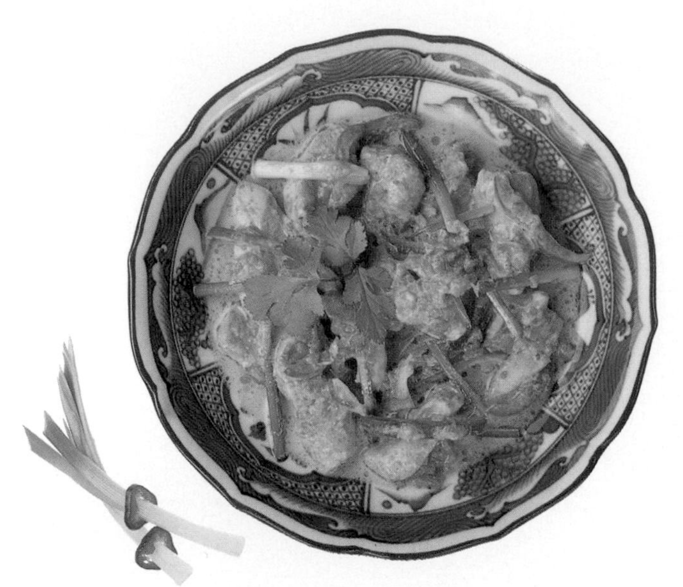

THAI CURRY

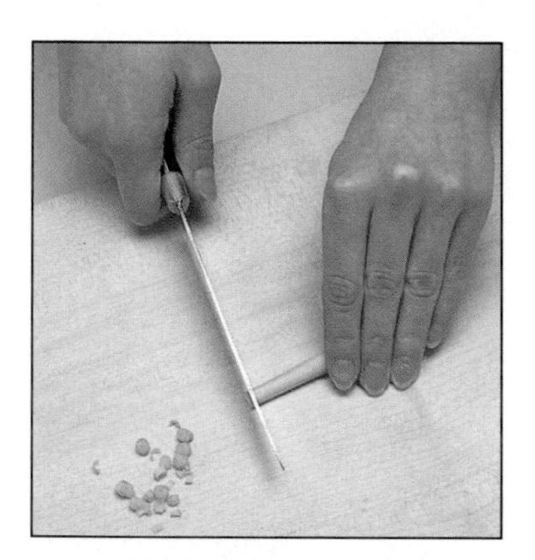

1 small onion, chopped
1 clove garlic, peeled
1 blade lemon grass, chopped
1 teaspoon ground coriander
½ teaspoon dried chilli flakes
1 teaspoon grated lime rind
1 teaspoon paprika
½ teaspoon ground cumin
2 teaspoons vegetable oil
450 g (1 lb) raw chicken meat, sliced
3 teaspoons light soy sauce
150 ml (5 fl oz/⅔ cup) coconut milk
2 lime leaves
55 ml (2 fl oz/¼ cup) chicken stock
2 red peppers (capsicums), deseeded and sliced
10 spring onions, sliced into matchstick strips

Blend or process the first 8 ingredients in a blender or food processor until smooth. Heat the oil in a large frying pan, stir in the paste and cook for 1-2 minutes. Add the chicken and stir gently, coating well in the curry paste.

Stir in the soy sauce, coconut milk, lime leaves, chicken stock, peppers (capsicums) and spring onions. Cover and cook for 20-25 minutes. Serve with plain boiled rice and garnish with sprigs of coriander.

Serves 4.

SWEET & SOUR CHICKEN

700 g (1½ lb) skinned and boned chicken breasts
salt
5 tablespoons cornflour
225 g (8 oz/2 cups) self-raising flour
3 large eggs, beaten
2.5 cm (1 in) piece fresh root ginger, finely chopped
1 tablespoon oil, plus extra for frying
100 ml (3½ fl oz/⅓ cup) white wine vinegar
55 ml (2 fl oz/¼ cup) dry sherry
100 ml (3½ fl oz/⅓ cup) orange juice
3 tablespoons soy sauce
4 tablespoons tomato purée (paste)
1 clove garlic, finely chopped
1 small onion, finely chopped
1 red pepper (capsicum), sliced
1 green pepper (capsicum), sliced

Cut the chicken into 2.5 cm (1 in) cubes. Sprinkle with salt and 2 tablespoons cornflour and mix thoroughly. Meanwhile, make the batter. Put the flour in a bowl, gradually add the eggs and 300 ml (10 fl oz/1¼ cups) water to make a smooth batter. Add half the ginger. Add the chicken and coat thoroughly. Half-fill a deep fat pan or fryer with oil and heat to 190C (375F). Add the chicken, in batches, and fry for 4-5 minutes until crispy. Remove with a slotted spoon, drain and transfer to a plate to keep warm.

In a jug, mix remaining 3 tablespoons cornflour with 150 ml (5 fl oz/⅔ cup) water, then add the wine vinegar, sherry, orange juice, soy sauce and tomato purée (paste). Heat 1 tablespoon oil in a wok or large frying pan, add the garlic and the rest of the ginger, stir-fry for 15 seconds. Add the onion and peppers (capsicums) and stir-fry for 1½-2 minutes, then pour over the sauce, stirring until it thickens. Put the chicken on a warm serving dish and pour over the sauce.

Serves 4-6.

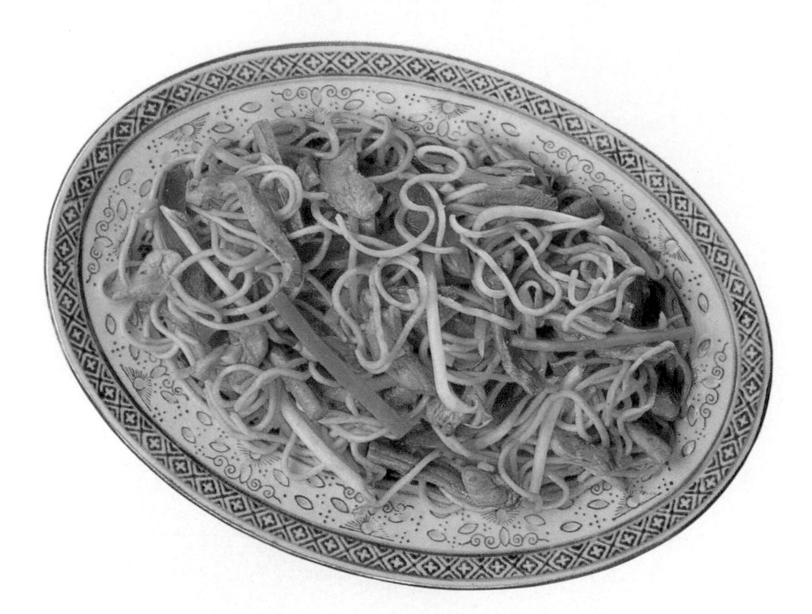

CHICKEN CHOW MEIN

3 tablespoons dark soy sauce
2 tablespoons dry sherry
1 teaspoon soft brown sugar
1 teaspoon sweet chilli sauce
225 g (8 oz) skinned and boned chicken, shredded
225 g (8 oz) egg thread noodles
1 teaspoon cornflour
6 tablespoons chicken stock or water
3 tablespoons vegetable oil
2.5 cm (1 in) piece fresh root ginger, finely chopped
1 clove garlic, finely chopped
4 spring onions, sliced
85 g (3 oz) green beans, cut into 2.5 cm (1 in) lengths
1 small carrot, cut into matchstick strips
1 red pepper (capsicum), finely sliced
175 g (6 oz) beansprouts

In a bowl, mix together soy sauce, sherry, brown sugar and chilli sauce. Add the chicken and leave to marinate for 30 minutes. Drain the chicken, reserving the marinade. Cook the noodles following the packet instructions; drain and set aside. Mix the reserved marinade with the cornflour and chicken stock or water and set aside.

In a wok or large frying pan, heat the oil, add the ginger and garlic and stir-fry for 15-20 seconds, then add the chicken and continue to stir-fry for further 2-3 minutes until the chicken is cooked. Add the spring onions, beans, carrot and pepper (capsicum) and stir-fry for 1 minute. Add the noodles and beansprouts and stir-fry for 30 seconds, then add the marinade mixture and stir-fry until the sauce thickens and coats the ingredients. Serve immediately.

Serves 4.

CHICKEN & BLACK BEAN SAUCE

1 teaspoon cornflour
4 teaspoons light soy sauce
2.5 cm (1 in) piece fresh root ginger, finely chopped
1 clove garlic, crushed
350 g (12 oz) skinned and boned chicken breasts
1 green pepper (capsicum), deseeded
8 canned water chestnuts, drained
4 spring onions
2 tablespoons vegetable oil
55 g (2 oz/½ cup) cashew nuts
5 tablespoons dry sherry
175 g (6 oz) bottle black bean sauce

In a bowl, mix together the cornflour, soy sauce, ginger and garlic. Slice the chicken into thin strips and coat in the cornflour mixture and leave to stand for 10 minutes. Dice the green pepper (capsicum), cut the water chestnuts in half and slice the spring onions into 2.5 cm (1 in) lengths; set aside.

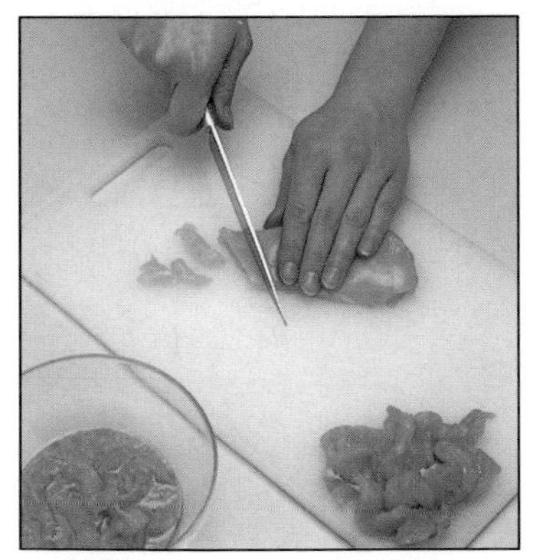

In a wok or large frying pan, heat the oil, add the chicken and stir-fry for 2 minutes, then add the pepper (capsicum), spring onions and water chestnuts and stir-fry for a further 1 minute. Add the cashew nuts, sherry and black bean sauce and stir-fry until sauce thickens.

Serves 4.

ARABIAN POUSSIN

3 teaspoons olive oil
1 small red onion, finely chopped
225 g (8 oz/1¼ cups) couscous
350 ml (12 fl oz/1½ cups) chicken stock
25 g (1 oz) no-need-to-soak dried apricots, finely chopped
15 g (½ oz/2 tablespoons) raisins
grated rind and juice of ½ lemon
25 g (1 oz/¼ cup) toasted pine nuts
1 tablespoon chopped fresh mint
4 poussins
salt and pepper
150 ml (5 fl oz/⅔ cup) dry white wine
2 teaspoons mint jelly

Preheat oven to 180C (350F/Gas 4). In a pan, heat 1 tablespoon oil and gently fry the onion until soft. Put the couscous into a bowl and add 225 ml (8 fl oz/1 cup) of the stock, the fried onion, apricots, raisins and the lemon rind and juice and leave to stand for 15 minutes. Stir in the pine nuts and mint. Loosen the skin around the breast of each poussin and carefully push the stuffing round the meat, securing the skin in place with a wooden cocktail stick. Use any excess stuffing to place under the poussins in a roasting tin.

Brush the poussins with the remaining oil and sprinkle with salt and black pepper. Roast in the oven for 50-60 minutes, basting occasionally. Remove the poussins from the roasting tin and set aside. Pour the remaining stock, wine and mint jelly into the pan and stir together over a high heat, bring to the boil and spoon over the poussins.

Serves 4.

TIKKA KEBABS

150 ml (5 fl oz/2⁄3 cup) natural yogurt
1 tablespoon grated fresh root ginger
2 cloves garlic, crushed
1 teaspoon chilli powder
1 teaspoon ground cumin
1 teaspoon tumeric
1 tablespoon coriander seeds
juice of 1 lemon
1⁄2 teaspoon salt
2 tablespoons chopped fresh coriander
350 g (12 oz) chicken meat, cubed
RAITA:
150 ml (5 fl oz/2⁄3 cup) natural yogurt
2 teaspoons mint jelly
85 g (3 oz) finely chopped cucumber
2 spring onions, finely chopped

Blend the first 10 ingredients in a blender or food processor until smooth. Pour into a bowl. Stir in the cubed chicken, cover and allow to stand overnight in the refrigerator.

Preheat grill. Thread chicken onto skewers and cook under the hot grill for 15-20 minutes, turning frequently and brushing with any remaining marinade. In a bowl, mix together the raita ingredients. Serve the kebabs on a bed of pilau rice, garnished with sprigs of coriander and lemon wedges. Hand the raita separately.

Serves 4.

CHICKEN BIRYANI

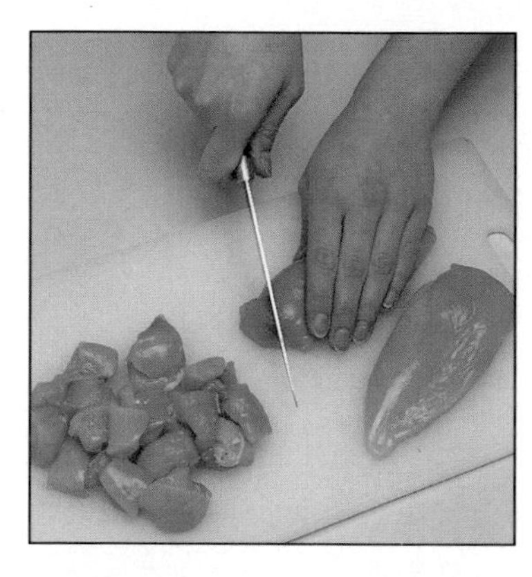

8 tablespoons vegetable oil
1 stick cinnamon
8 cloves
6 cardamom pods, bruised
2.5 cm (1 in) piece fresh root ginger, finely chopped
700 g (1½ lb) skinned and boned chicken, cubed
2 cloves garlic, crushed
1 teaspoon chilli powder
300 ml (10 fl oz/1¼ cups) natural yogurt
150 ml (5 fl oz/⅔ cup) chicken stock
pinch of saffron strands
4 tablespoons boiling water
350 g (12 oz/2¼ cups) basmati rice
4 tablespoons sultanas
4 tablespoons flaked almonds
1 onion, sliced

Preheat oven to 190C (375F/Gas 5). In a flameproof casserole, heat 4 tablespoons oil and add the spices and fry for 15 seconds. Add the chicken, garlic and chilli and fry for 4 minutes. Add the yogurt, 1 tablespoon at a time, stirring between each addition until yogurt is absorbed by the spices. Add the stock and simmer for 20-25 minutes. Transfer to a bowl. Soak the saffron in the boiling water and put to one side. Wash the rice under cold running water until the water runs clear, then cook in boiling, salted water for 3 minutes and drain.

Put 2 tablespoons oil in the casserole, spoon in a layer of rice, sprinkle with a little of the saffron water and cover with a layer of chicken. Repeat, ending with a layer of rice. Add any cooking juices left from the chicken, cover tightly and cook in the oven for 25-30 minutes. In a pan, heat the remaining oil and fry the sultanas and almonds until golden; remove. Fry the onions until crisp and golden. Sprinkle the biryani with the almonds, onions and sultanas.

Serves 4.

MUGHLAI CHICKEN

6 cloves garlic, peeled
85 g (3 oz) blanched almonds
2.5 cm (1 in) piece root ginger, peeled and chopped
6 tablespoons vegetable oil
1 kg (2¼ lb) chicken pieces
9 whole cardamom pods
1 stick cinamon
6 whole cloves
1 onion, finely chopped
2½ teaspoons ground cumin
1 teaspoon cayenne pepper
150 ml (5 fl oz/⅔ cup) natural yogurt
300 ml (10 fl oz/1¼ cups) double (thick) cream
1 tablespoon sultanas
1 firm, ripe banana
½ teaspoon each garam masala and salt

Put the garlic, almonds, ginger and 4 tablespoons water into a blender and blend to form a paste. Cube chicken. Heat the oil in a flameproof casserole or saucepan and fry the chicken on both sides until golden. Set aside. Put the cardamom, cinnamon and cloves into the pan and fry for a few seconds. Add the chopped onion and fry until beginning to turn golden brown. Add the paste from the blender together with the cumin and cayenne and fry for 2 minutes or until the mixture is lightly browned.

Still on the heat, add 1 tablespoon yogurt and cook for about 20 seconds, then add another tablespoon. Continue adding yogurt in this way until it has all been added. Put the chicken pieces and any juices into the pan with the salt and cream and gently bring to a simmer, stirring. Cover and leave to cook gently for about 20 minutes. Add the sultanas and banana and cook for a further 10 minutes or until the chicken is tender. Stir in the garam masala and salt.

Serves 4.

CACCIATORE

2 tablespoons olive oil
4 large chicken breasts, with bones
175 g (6 oz) red onion, thinly sliced
2 cloves garlic, thinly sliced
150 ml (5 fl oz/⅔ cup) red wine
150 ml (5 fl oz/⅔ cup) chicken stock
400 g (14 oz) can chopped tomatoes
3 teaspoons tomato purée (paste)
1 red pepper (capsicum), deseeded and sliced
1 yellow pepper (capsicum), deseeded and sliced
2 tablespoons chopped fresh basil
salt and pepper
pinch of sugar
pasta noodles, to serve

Preheat oven to 180C (350F/Gas 4). In a pan, heat the oil and fry the chicken breasts all over until golden brown, then transfer to a shallow casserole. Gently fry the onion and garlic in the pan without browning, add the wine, stock, tomatoes, tomato purée (paste), pepper (capsicum), 1 tablespoon of the basil, salt and pepper and the sugar and bring to the boil.

Pour over the chicken, cover and cook in the oven for 45 minutes. Serve on a bed of pasta noodles and sprinkle with the remaining basil and plenty of black pepper.

Serves 4.

CIDER APPLE CHICKEN

pared rind of 1 lemon plus 1 teaspoon juice
½ cinnamon stick
1 onion, quartered
1.5 kg (3¼-3½ lb) chicken
salt and pepper
85 g (3 oz/⅓ cup) butter
1 tablespoon oil
3 tablespoons brandy
450 g (1 lb) eating apples, peeled and cored
150 ml (5 fl oz/⅔ cup) cider
300 ml (10 fl oz/1¼ cups) crème fraîche
1 tablespoon each chopped fresh chives and parsley

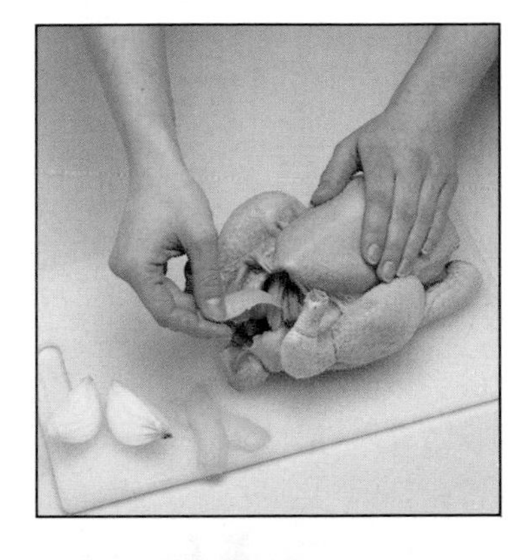

Place rind, cinnamon stick and onion in the chicken. Season well.

Preheat oven to 180C (350F/Gas 4). Heat 55 g (2 oz/¼ cup) butter and the oil in a flameproof casserole and brown the chicken on all sides. Pour over the brandy and ignite. Thinly slice one of the apples and add to the casserole once the flames have died down. Add the cider to the casserole, bring to the boil, cover and cook in the oven for 1¼ hours.

Melt the remaining butter in a pan, cut the remaining apples into thick slices and sauté until just cooked. Remove the chicken from the casserole and place on a warmed serving platter and surround with the sautéed apples. Add the crème fraîche and lemon juice to the casserole, stir well and boil to reduce slightly. Season well and pour over the chicken. Sprinkle with the chopped herbs and serve at once.

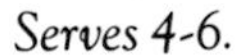

Serves 4-6.

CHICKEN & VEGETABLES

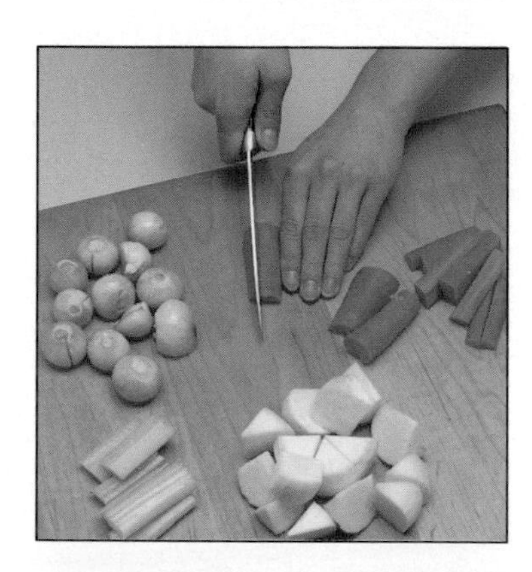

1 tablespoon oil
115 g (4 oz) smoked bacon, chopped
2 cloves garlic, peeled
12 shallots, peeled
1 stick celery, cut into 2.5 cm (1 in) lengths
2 small turnips, peeled and quartered
2 carrots, peeled and cut into matchstick strips
225 g (8 oz) button mushrooms
150 ml (5 fl oz/⅔ cup) dry white wine
150 ml (5 fl oz/⅔ cup) chicken stock
1.35 kg (3 lb) corn-fed chicken, without giblets
55 ml (2 fl oz/¼ cup) double (thick) cream
juice of ½ lemon
salt and pepper

Preheat oven to 200C (400F/Gas 6). In a flameproof casserole, heat the oil, add the bacon, garlic and shallots and fry for 2-3 minutes. Add the remaining vegetables and fry for a further 2-3 minutes until the bacon is starting to turn golden brown. Pour the wine over the vegetables and boil rapidly to reduce the liquid by half. Add the chicken stock. Remove the casserole from the heat and add the chicken. Cover and cook in the oven for 45-55 minutes.

To check if the chicken is cooked, pierce the leg with a skewer: it is ready if the juices run clear; if not return to the oven for a further few minutes before testing again. When cooked, remove the chicken and vegetables to a serving dish. Cover and keep warm. Return the casserole to the heat, skim off any fat and boil vigorously to reduce to just over 150 ml (5 fl oz/⅔ cup). Add the cream and simmer for 2 minutes; add the lemon juice and salt and pepper. Serve hot with the chicken.

Serves 4.

CASSOULET

225 g (8 oz/1 ¼ cups) haricot beans, soaked overnight
700 ml (25 fl oz/3 ¼ cups) chicken stock
2 tablespoons olive oil
8 chicken thighs
115 g (4 oz) smoked rindless bacon, cut into strips
1 large onion, thinly sliced
2 cloves garlic, thinly sliced
150 ml (5 fl oz/⅔ cup) dry white wine
200 g (7 oz) can chopped tomatoes
2 tablespoons tomato purée (paste)
1 bouquet garni
salt and pepper
225 g (8 oz) chorizo sausage, cut into large chunks
25 g (1 oz/6 teaspoons) butter
55 g (2 oz/1 cup) fresh white breadcrumbs
2 tablespoons chopped fresh parsley

Drain the beans and put into a large pan with 550 ml (20 fl oz/2½ cups) of the stock and enough water to cover. Bring to the boil and simmer for 50 minutes. Preheat oven to 180C (350F/Gas 4). Heat 1 tablespoon oil and fry the chicken until golden, then remove from the pan and set aside. Fry the bacon until browned, then add the onion and garlic and continue cooking until softened. Drain the beans and return to the pan with the wine, remaining stock, tomatoes, tomato purée (paste), bouquet garni and seasonings. Bring to the boil, then stir in the bacon mixture.

Transfer half the bean mixture to a flameproof casserole. Arrange the chicken and chorizo on top and cover with the remaining beans. Cover and bring to the boil, then transfer to the oven and cook for 1 hour. Melt the butter and remaining oil in a frying pan and fry the breadcrumbs until golden. Stir in the parsley. Uncover the casserole, sprinkle over the breadcrumbs and return to the oven. Cook for a further 15-20 minutes. Serve with bread and a salad.

Serves 4.

MOROCCAN CHICKEN

3 cloves garlic, crushed, or 1 tablespoon garlic paste
1 teaspoon each paprika and ground ginger
½ teaspoon ground cumin
4 tablespoons olive oil
4 skinned and boned chicken breasts
1 large onion, finely chopped
4 tablespoons chopped fresh parsley
pinch of saffron threads
150 ml (5 fl oz/⅔ cup) chicken stock
12 green olives
finely grated rind and juice of ½ lemon
salt and pepper

Mix the garlic, paprika, ginger and cumin with 3 tablespoons olive oil.

Place the chicken portions in a shallow dish and pour over the oil and spices and leave to marinate for 3-4 hours. Heat the remaining oil in a pan, add the onion and cook gently for 2-3 minutes. Add the chicken pieces and the marinade to the pan and brown the chicken slightly. Add the parsley, saffron and chicken stock; cover and simmer for 30 minutes or until the chicken is cooked.

Remove chicken from the pan and keep warm. Add the olives and lemon rind and juice and season with a little salt and pepper. Bring to the boil and boil rapidly until reduced to approximately 150 ml (5 fl oz/⅔ cup). Pour over the chicken and serve immediately.

Serves 4.

LENTIL-BAKED CHICKEN

225 g (8 oz/1 ¼ cups) green lentils
25 g (1 oz/6 teaspoons) butter
1 tablespoon olive oil
1.5 kg (3¼-3½ lb) chicken
175 g (6 oz) smoked streaky bacon
12 shallots, halved
4 cloves garlic, thickly sliced
150 ml (5 fl oz/⅔ cup) dry white wine
300 ml (10 fl oz/1 ¼ cups) chicken stock
1 bouquet garni
chopped fresh parsley, to garnish

Preheat oven to 200C (400F/Gas 6). Place the lentils in a pan of salted water, bring to the boil and simmer for 15 minutes.

In a flameproof casserole, heat the butter and oil and brown the chicken on all sides, then remove from the casserole and set aside. Cut the bacon into thick strips and add to the casserole with the shallots and garlic and cook for 2-3 minutes. Drain the lentils and stir into the bacon mixture, place the chicken on the bed of lentils, pour over the wine and stock and add the bouquet garni. Bring to the boil, cover and cook in the oven for 50 minutes.

Remove the lid of the casserole, add a little water if the lentil mixture is looking too dry and return to the oven, uncovered, for a further 35-40 minutes until the juices of the chicken run clear when pierced. Remove the bouquet garni and garnish with chopped fresh parsley.

Serves 4-6.

FAMILY CHICKEN PIE

700 g (1½ lb) chicken pieces
1 large onion, thickly sliced
85 ml (3 fl oz/⅓ cup) dry white wine
200 ml (7 fl oz/¾ cup) chicken stock
1 bouquet garni and salt and pepper
25 g (1 oz/6 teaspoons) butter
175 g (6 oz) button mushrooms, halved
25 g (1 oz/¼ cup) plain flour
225 g (8 oz) can sweetcorn kernels
2 tablespoons chopped fresh parsley
1 teaspoon lemon juice
4 tablespoons double (thick) cream
1 kg (2 lb) potatoes
115 ml (4 fl oz/½ cup) hot milk
85 g (3 oz/¾ cup) grated Cheddar cheese
25 g (1 oz) salted potato crisps, crushed

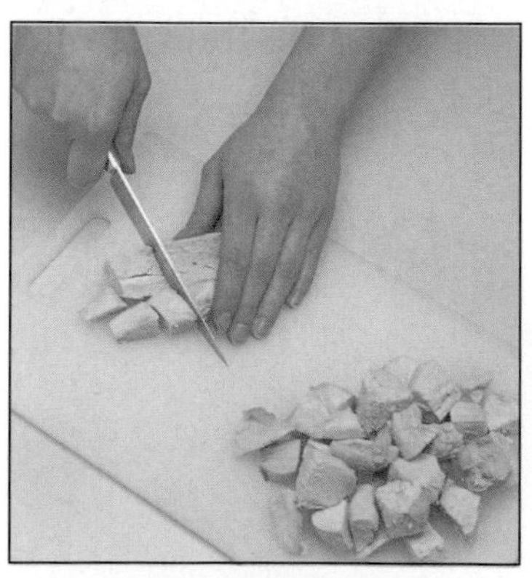

Place the chicken, onion, wine, stock and bouquet garni in a large pan and bring to the boil. Reduce the heat and simmer for 25-30 minutes until the chicken is tender. Drain the liquid and reserve for the sauce. Discard the bouquet garni and remove skin and bones from the chicken; coarsely chop the flesh. Melt the butter in a pan and gently fry the mushrooms, then stir in the flour and cook for 1 minute. Add the reserved poaching liquor and onion.

Return to the heat and bring to the boil, stirring continuously. Stir in the chicken, sweetcorn, parsley, lemon juice and cream and season to taste with salt and pepper. Cook the potatoes and mash with the milk and 55 g (2 oz/½ cup) of the cheese and season to taste. Preheat grill. Spoon the chicken mixture into a flameproof dish and cover with creamed potato. Mix the crisps with the remaining cheese. Sprinkle over the potato crisps and grill until golden.

Serves 4.

CHICKEN & HAM PIE

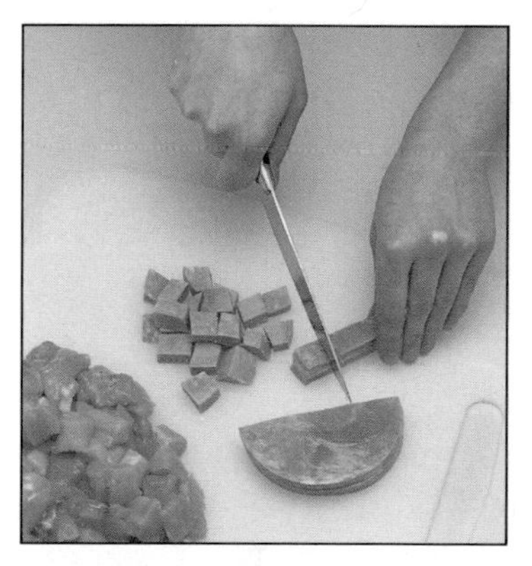

25 g (1 oz/6 teaspoons) butter
225 g (8 oz) sweetcure ham, cut into 2.5 cm (1 in) cubes
350 g (12 oz) skinned and boned chicken, cut into 2.5 cm (1 in) cubes
1 onion, chopped
225 g (8 oz) leeks, trimmed and sliced
175 g (6 oz) button mushrooms, sliced
25 g (1 oz/¼ cup) plain flour
300 ml (10 fl oz/1¼ cups) chicken stock
150 ml (5 fl oz/⅔ cup) single (light) cream
finely grated rind of ½ lemon
salt and pepper
225 g (8 oz) shortcrust pastry
2 tablespoons grated Parmesan cheese
milk for glazing

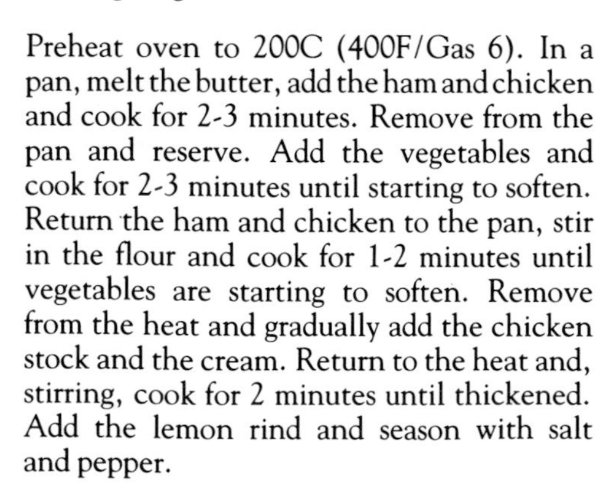

Preheat oven to 200C (400F/Gas 6). In a pan, melt the butter, add the ham and chicken and cook for 2-3 minutes. Remove from the pan and reserve. Add the vegetables and cook for 2-3 minutes until starting to soften. Return the ham and chicken to the pan, stir in the flour and cook for 1-2 minutes until vegetables are starting to soften. Remove from the heat and gradually add the chicken stock and the cream. Return to the heat and, stirring, cook for 2 minutes until thickened. Add the lemon rind and season with salt and pepper.

Transfer the chicken and ham mixture to a 1 litre (35 fl oz/4½ cup) pie dish. Mix the pastry with the Parmesan, then roll out on a floured surface 2.5 cm (1 in) larger than the pie dish. Cut off a 2.5 cm (1 in) strip to fit the edge of the dish. Brush the edge with a little water, then cover with the pastry lid. Pinch the edges together to seal and brush the pie with milk to glaze. Bake in the oven for 25-30 minutes or until the pastry is golden brown.

Serves 4.

CHICKEN & MUSHROOM COBBLER

25 g (1 oz/6 teaspoons) butter
1 small onion, finely chopped
225 g (8 oz) button mushrooms, sliced
25 g (1 oz/¼ cup) plain flour
200 ml (7 fl oz/¾ cup) chicken stock
200 ml (7 fl oz/¾ cup) single (light) cream
450 g (1 lb) cooked chicken, diced
salt and pepper
2 tablespoons chopped fresh parsley
FOR THE SCONE DOUGH:
115 g (4 oz/1 cup) plain flour
55 g (2 oz/¼ cup) butter
25 g (1 oz/¼ cup) grated Cheddar cheese
3 tablespoons cold milk

Preheat oven to 190C (375F/Gas 5). In a large pan, heat the butter, add the onion and mushrooms and cook for 2-3 minutes until the vegetables start to soften. Sprinkle over the flour and cook for 1 minute. Gradually blend in the stock and the cream. Return the pan to the heat and cook for 2 minutes, stirring until the sauce thickens.

Add the chicken, season and add the parsley; mix well. Transfer to an ovenproof dish. Sift the flour into a bowl, rub in the butter finely, then stir in the cheese and mix with enough milk to form a soft, but not sticky, dough. On a floured surface, roll the dough out to a thickness of 2.5 cm (1 in) then, with a fluted cutter, cut out 12 rounds. Arrange these around the edge of the dish and brush with a little milk. Bake in the oven for 35-40 minutes until golden. Serve hot.

Serves 4.

CHICKEN & FETA PIE

225 g (8 oz) cooked minced chicken
350 g (12 oz) frozen spinach leaves, defrosted, well drained and chopped
175 g (6 oz) feta cheese
1 teaspoon finely grated lemon rind
2 teaspoons lemon juice
¼ teaspoon freshly grated nutmeg
freshly ground black pepper
6 sheets filo pastry
45 g (1½ oz/9 teaspoons) butter, melted

Preheat oven to 200C (400F/Gas 6). In a large bowl, mix together the chicken, spinach, feta, lemon rind and juice, nutmeg and pepper.

Brush one of the sheets of filo pastry with butter and press it gently into a 27.5 x 17.5 cm (11 x 7 in) non-stick tin, allowing the ends of the pastry to overlap the tin. Repeat with a second sheet of pastry, placed at a 90° angle; repeat with 2 more sheets of pastry, brushing with butter each time.

Spoon the spinach filling into the filo case and bring the overlapping pastry sides over the filling. Crumple the remaining pastry and arrange loosely on top of the pie. Brush lightly with any remaining butter and cook in the oven for 25-30 minutes until golden and crisp.

Serves 4-6.

CHICKEN PASTIES

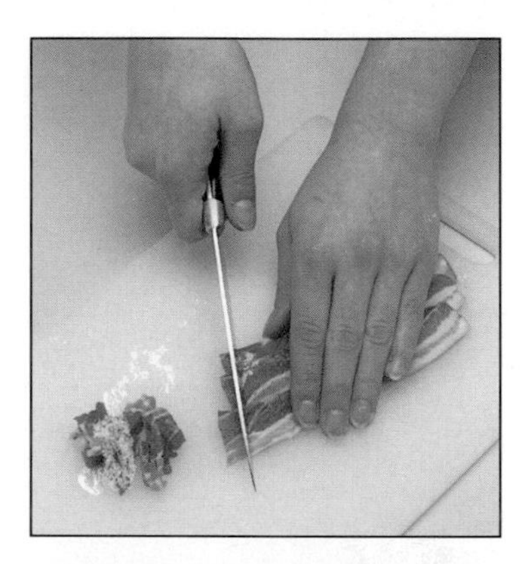

350 g (12 oz/3 cups) plain flour
salt and pepper
85 g (3 oz/⅓ cup) butter
85 g (3 oz/⅓ cup) solid vegetable fat
1 tablespoon fresh chopped thyme
1 tablespoon vegetable oil
½ onion, chopped
55 g (2 oz) rindless streaky bacon, chopped
1 carrot, peeled and diced
1 large potato, peeled and diced
350 g (12 oz) chicken breast, minced
85 g (3 oz) mushrooms, chopped
½ tablespoon plain flour
150 ml (5 fl oz/⅔ cup) chicken stock
beaten egg or milk for brushing

Preheat oven to 190C (375F/Gas 5). Sift the flour and a pinch of salt into a bowl, add fats and rub in finely until mixture resembles breadcrumbs. Add the chopped thyme and 3 tablespoons iced water and mix together to form a dough. Wrap in cling film and refrigerate for 30 minutes. Heat the oil in a frying pan and add the onion, bacon, carrot and potato and fry for 2-3 minutes until the onion starts to soften. Add the chicken and mushrooms and fry for a further 3-4 minutes. Add the flour and cook for 1 minute.

Gradually add the stock, return to the heat and, stirring, cook for 2 minutes until the sauce thickens. Season and leave to cool. On a floured surface, roll out the pastry and cut out eight 15 cm (6 in) rounds. Place 2 tablespoons of the cold mixture in the centre of each round, brush the edges with a little beaten egg or milk and fold the pastry over to enclose the filling. Pinch the edges together to seal. Glaze with egg or milk and place on a baking sheet. Bake for 20-25 minutes until golden.

Serves 4.

STUFFED CHICKEN PARCELS

4 skinned and boned chicken breasts
115 g (4 oz) duck liver pâté
1 teaspoon finely grated orange rind
3 teaspoons orange juice
5 sprigs of thyme
salt and pepper
25 g (1 oz/6 teaspoons) butter
2 teaspoons olive oil
350 g (12 oz) ready-made puff pastry
1 large egg, beaten
1 teaspoon poppy seeds

Preheat the oven to 200C (400F/Gas 6). Cut a small incision in each chicken breast to make a pocket.

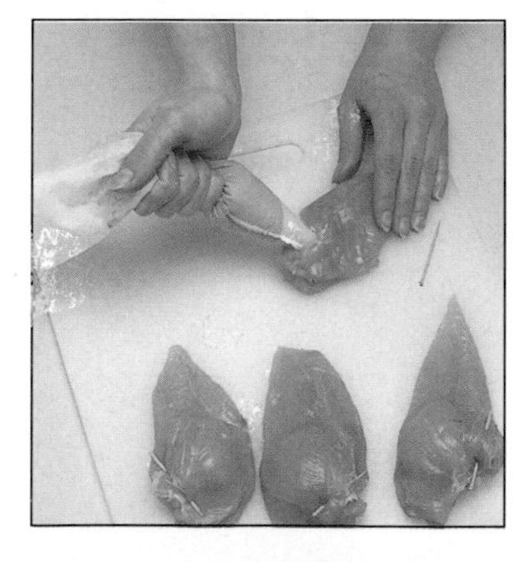

Mix together the pâté, orange rind and juice, 1 sprig of finely chopped thyme and seasoning. Transfer the mixture to a piping bag fitted with a plain nozzle and pipe a quarter of the mixture into each pocket and seal with a wooden cocktail stick. In a frying pan, heat the butter and oil and seal the chicken quickly on both sides until well browned. Remove from the heat, drain and cool, then chill. Thinly roll out the pastry and cut into long 4 cm (1½ in) wide strips. Discard the cocktail sticks from the chicken and top each breast with a sprig of thyme.

Brush the pastry strips with egg and wind the strips, egg-side in, around the breasts, overlapping very slightly to enclose the chicken completely. Place on a lightly dampened baking sheet, brush with remaining egg and sprinkle with poppy seeds. Make a small hole in the top of each one and bake in the oven for 35-40 minutes until golden. Serve with buttered new potatoes and an orange salad.

Serves 4.

PUFF PASTRY ROLLS

1 tablespoon oil
2 shallots, finely chopped
1 clove garlic, crushed
115 g (4 oz) mushrooms, finely chopped
1 tablespoon chopped fresh sage
1 tablespoon chopped fresh thyme
225 g (8 oz) skinned and boned chicken
2 tablespoons Greek yogurt
2 tablespoons grated Parmesan cheese
salt and pepper
175 g (6 oz) ready-made puff pastry
1 egg, beaten

Preheat oven to 200C (400F/Gas 6). Heat the oil in a small pan, add the shallots, garlic and mushrooms and fry for 3-4 minutes until soft. Add the chopped herbs and put to one side to cool. Finely mince the chicken, transfer to a bowl and add the yogurt, 1 tablespoon Parmesan cheese, the shallot and mushroom mixture and season with a little salt and pepper; mix well. On a floured surface, roll out the puff pastry to a rectangle measuring about 30 x 40 cm (12 x 16 in) and cut into 4 strips lengthways.

Place spoonfuls of the mixture along the length of each strip. Brush the edges with a little beaten egg and fold the pastry over to enclose the filling. Pinch the edges of the pastry together to seal. Brush with a little more beaten egg and sprinkle with the remaining Parmesan cheese. Cut into 5 cm (2 in) lengths and make 2 slashes in each roll. Place on a greased baking sheet and bake in the oven for 15-20 minutes or until golden brown.

Serves 4.

CHICKEN & TOMATO PIE

225 g (8 oz/2 cups) plain flour
pinch of salt
55 g (2 oz/¼ cup) unsalted butter, chilled and cubed
55 g (2 oz/¼ cup) white vegetable fat, chilled and cubed
2 tablespoons iced water
450 g (1 lb) cooked chicken, skinned and boned
6 tomatoes, sliced
300 ml (10 fl oz/1¼ cups) thick sour cream
3 tablespoons pesto sauce
salt and pepper
beaten egg or milk for glazing

Preheat oven to 190C (375F/Gas 5). To make the pastry, sift the flour and salt into a bowl, add the butter and vegetable fat and rub in finely until the mixture resembles breadcrumbs. Add the water and mix together with a knife until the dough forms a ball. Wrap in cling film and refrigerate for 30 minutes. Cut the chicken into slices and layer with the tomatoes in a 20 cm (8 in) dish, filling almost to the top. Mix together the thick sour cream and pesto, season with a little salt and pepper and pour over the chicken and tomatoes.

Roll out the pastry and, using the pie dish as a guide, cut out a piece slightly larger than the dish. Roll out the trimmings, and cut a strip to place on the rim of the pie dish, then brush with a little water. Place the pastry lid on top. Pinch the edges together to seal and brush the surface of pie with a little beaten egg or milk to glaze. Cook in the oven for 25-30 minutes or until the pastry is golden and crisp. This pie is delicious eaten cold.

Serves 4.

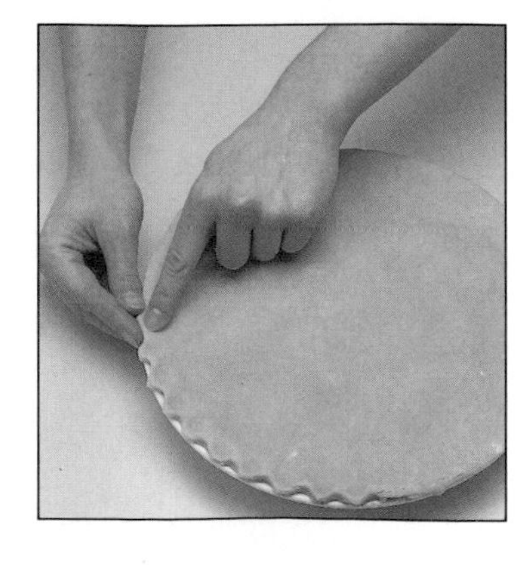

ROQUEFORT VERONIQUE

25 g (1 oz/6 teaspoons) butter
1 tablespoon oil
4 skinned and boned chicken breasts
1 leek, trimmed and chopped
2 teaspoons plain flour
175 ml (6 fl oz/¾ cup) milk
70 g (2½ oz) Roquefort cheese
85 ml (3 fl oz/⅓ cup) single (light) cream
150 g (5 oz) seedless green grapes, skinned
chopped fresh parsley, to garnish

In a frying pan, heat the butter and oil and cook the chicken on all sides until golden.

Reduce the heat, stir in the chopped leek, cover and continue cooking for 30 minutes until the juices of the chicken run clear when pierced. Remove the chicken from the pan and set aside on a warmed serving plate.

Sprinkle the flour into the pan and cook for 1 minute, remove from the heat and gradually add the milk. Return to the heat and stirring bring to the boil and cook for 2 minutes until thickened. Add the cheese, cream and grapes and cook for a further 5 minutes, stirring all the time. Pour over the chicken and garnish with chopped fresh parsley.

Serves 4.

CHICKEN STROGANOFF

450 g (1 lb) skinned and boned chicken breasts
55 g (2 oz/¼ cup) butter
1 tablespoon olive oil
2 onions, thinly sliced
175 g (6 oz) button mushrooms, sliced
2 teaspoons Dijon mustard
55 g (2 oz) gherkins, sliced
200 ml (7 fl oz/¾ cup) thick sour cream
salt and pepper
noodles or rice, to serve
chopped fresh parsley and paprika, to garnish

Place the chicken between 2 sheets of cling film. Use a rolling pin to flatten. Slice into 1 x 4 cm (½ x 1½ in) strips.

In a frying pan, heat the half the butter and oil and cook the onions until softened. Add the mushrooms and cook for a further 5 minutes Remove from the pan and set aside.

Heat the remaining butter and oil in the pan and fry the chicken over a high heat, turning frequently, for 6-8 minutes until cooked. Return the onions and mushrooms to the pan, stir in the mustard, gherkins, cream and seasonings and heat through gently for 3-4 minutes. Serve on a bed of noodles or rice and garnish with chopped parsley and paprika.

Serves 4.

CHICKEN MOUSSELINE

FOR THE MOUSSE:
85 g (3 oz) watercress leaves
85 g (3 oz) chicken breast
salt and pepper
150 ml (5 fl oz/⅔ cup) double (thick) cream
8 chicken thighs, skinned and boned
FOR THE SAUCE:
1 tablespoon vegetable oil
1 shallot, finely chopped
150 ml (5 fl oz/⅔ cup) dry white wine
150 ml (5 fl oz/⅔ cup) chicken stock
55 ml (2 fl oz/¼ cup) double (thick) cream
1 teaspoon chopped fresh tarragon or basil
1 teaspoon lemon juice

To make the mousse, blanch the watercress in boiling, salted water for 15 seconds, drain and refresh under cold water. Drain again and squeeze as dry as possible.

Put the watercress into a food processor, add the chicken breast and season with a little salt and pepper. Process the mixture until very smooth. Gradually pour in the double cream while the processor is still running, taking care not to over-beat the mousse or the cream will separate and spoil the texture.

Preheat the oven to 190C (375F/Gas 5). Lay the chicken thighs on a board, season the insides with salt and pepper and add spoonfuls of the mousse. Roll the flesh around the mousse to enclose it and wrap each thigh in a square of oiled kitchen foil, sealing each one well. Place on a baking sheet and cook in the oven for 20-35 minutes or until the chicken is cooked and the mousse is firm.

Meanwhile, make the sauce. In a saucepan, heat the oil and gently fry the shallot until softened. Increase the heat, add the wine and boil rapidly until the quantity is reduced by half. Add the chicken stock and continue to boil to reduce the liquid until just under 150 ml (5 fl oz/⅔ cup) of stock remains.

With the stock at boiling point, add the cream and simmer for 3-4 minutes, stirring all the time, until the sauce starts to thicken. Add the tarragon and lemon juice and season with salt and pepper. Remove the chicken thighs from the foil and spoon over the sauce.

Serves 4.

— SMOKED CHICKEN KEDGEREE —

25 g (1 oz/6 teaspoons) butter
1 teaspoon coriander seeds, crushed
1 onion, sliced
1 teaspoon ground coriander
2 teaspoons ground cumin
85 g (3 oz/½ cup) long-grain rice
85 g (3 oz/½ cup) red lentils
550 ml (20 fl oz/2½ cups) chicken stock
350 g (12 oz) smoked chicken, coarsely chopped
juice of ½ lemon
115 ml (4 fl oz/½ cup) natural Greek yogurt
2 tablespoons chopped fresh parsley
2 hard-boiled eggs, coarsely chopped
1 lemon, sliced, to garnish
mango chutney and poppadoms, to serve

In a large pan, melt the butter, add the crushed coriander seeds and the onion and cook over a gentle heat until slightly softened, then stir in the ground coriander, cumin, rice and lentils and coat well with the butter. Pour in the stock, bring to the boil, then cover and simmer for 10 minutes.

Remove the lid, add the chicken and continue cooking for a further 10 minutes until all the liquid has been absorbed and the rice and lentils are tender. Stir in the lemon juice, yogurt, parsley and chopped hard-boiled eggs, and heat through gently. Spoon into a warmed serving dish and garnish with lemon. Serve with mango chutney and poppadoms.

Serves 4.

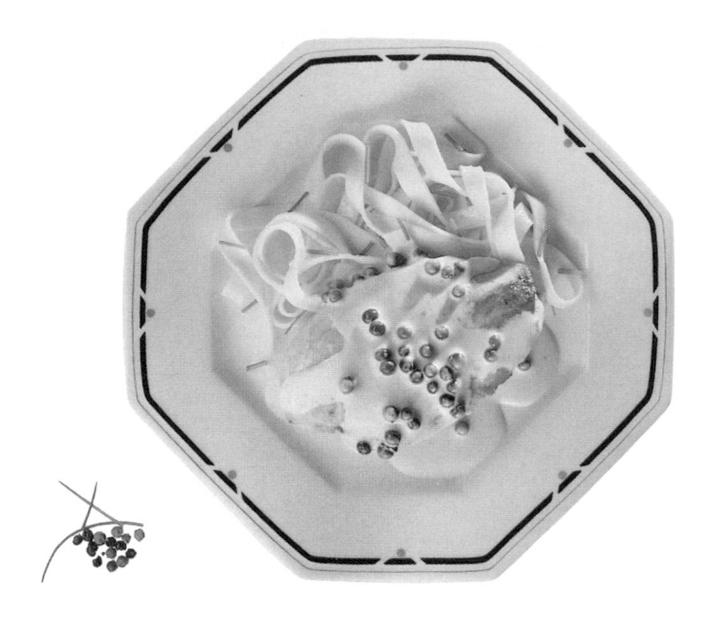

POULET AU POIVRE

25 g (1 oz/6 teaspoons) butter
1 tablespoon olive oil
4 skinned and boned chicken breasts
3 tablespoons brandy
250 ml (9 fl oz/1 cup) double (thick) cream
3 teaspoons pickled green peppercorns
3 teaspoons pickled pink peppercorns
pinch of sugar
salt

In a large frying pan, heat the butter and oil and fry the chicken breasts over a high heat to seal them all over.

Reduce the heat, cover and continue cooking for a further 25 minutes, turning regularly. Remove the chicken from the pan and set aside on a hot serving dish. Pour the brandy into the pan and ignite it using a lighted taper.

When the flames have died down, stir in the cream, peppercorns, sugar and salt, bring to the boil and simmer for 2-3 minutes. Pour over the chicken and serve at once.

Serves 4.

-CHICKEN WITH CHEESE SAUCE-

3 tablespoons vegetable oil
1 small onion, finely chopped
350 g (12 oz) chicken breast, sliced
150 g (5 oz) chestnut mushrooms
20 g (3/4 oz/9 teaspoons) plain flour
150 ml (5 fl oz/2/3 cup) dry white wine
150 ml (5 fl oz/2/3 cup) chicken stock or water
2 x 78 g (2 1/4 oz) Boursin cheeses with herbs and garlic
2 tablespoons chopped fresh parsley
salt and pepper
450 g (1 lb) fresh pasta

Heat 2 tablespoons oil and cook the onion until soft. Add the chicken and fry for 2 minutes. Add the mushrooms.

Fry for a further 2 minutes or until the chicken is cooked. Sprinkle over the flour and stir until all the fat is absorbed. Remove from the heat and slowly add the white wine and stock or water. Return the pan to the heat and bring to the boil, stirring, then reduce the heat and cook for 2 minutes, stirring until the sauce thickens.

Cut the cheese into cubes and add to the sauce, stirring until it has melted. Add the chopped parsley and season with a little salt and pepper. Cook the pasta in plenty of boiling salted water to which you have added the remaining tablespoon of oil (this prevents the pasta sticking together as it cooks) until just tender (*al dente*). Drain the pasta well and serve with the chicken sauce.

Serves 4.

PAELLA

25 g (1 oz/6 teaspoons) butter
1 tablespoon oil
4 chicken drumsticks or thighs
1 large onion, sliced
2 cloves garlic, crushed
1 red pepper (capsicum), deseeded and sliced
1 green pepper (capsicum), deseeded and sliced
175 g (6 oz/1 ¼ cups) long-grain rice
2 teaspoons paprika
550 ml (20 fl oz/2 ½ cups) chicken stock
pinch of saffron strands
175 g (6 oz) peeled prawns
175 g (6 oz) mussels, cleaned
85 g (3 oz) frozen peas
salt and pepper
chopped fresh parsley and lime wedges, to garnish

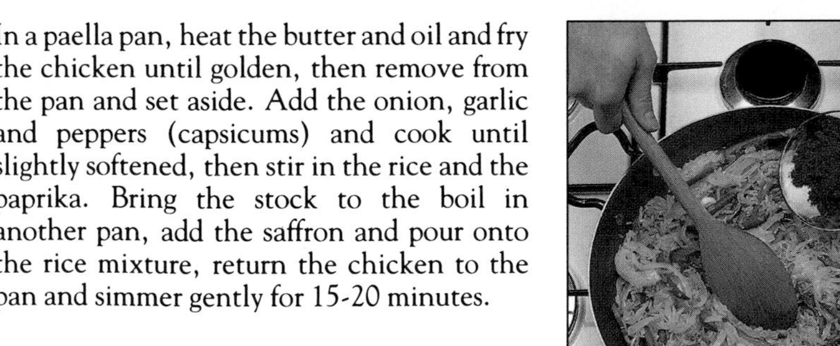

In a paella pan, heat the butter and oil and fry the chicken until golden, then remove from the pan and set aside. Add the onion, garlic and peppers (capsicums) and cook until slightly softened, then stir in the rice and the paprika. Bring the stock to the boil in another pan, add the saffron and pour onto the rice mixture, return the chicken to the pan and simmer gently for 15-20 minutes.

Add the prawns, mussels and peas and cook gently for a further 10 minutes or until all the liquid has been absorbed. Discard any mussels which remain closed. Season with plenty of salt and pepper and garnish with chopped parsley and wedges of lime.

Serves 4.

MUSHROOM RISOTTO

55 g (2 oz/¼ cup) butter
1 onion, finely chopped
225 g (8 oz) raw chicken meat, sliced into strips
55 g (2 oz) Parma ham, cut into strips
225 g (8 oz) mixed mushrooms, sliced
3 sprigs of rosemary
300 g (10 oz/2 cups) risotto rice
150 ml (5 fl oz/⅔ cup) white wine
850 ml (30 fl oz/3¾ cups) chicken stock
150 g (5 oz/1¼ cups) grated Mozzarella cheese
55 g (2 oz/½ cup) grated Parmesan cheese
salt and pepper

In a large pan, melt the butter and gently fry the onion until softened. Add the chicken and fry to seal quickly on all sides, then stir in the ham, mushrooms, rosemary and rice and cook until the rice is transparent.

Add the wine and cook, stirring continuously, until it has been absorbed. Pour in the stock, about 150 ml (5 fl oz/⅔ cup) at a time, stirring until it is absorbed. Continue adding the stock in this way until all the stock has been used up and the rice is creamy. Stir in the Mozzarella and continue cooking for a further 5 minutes. Serve at once, sprinkled with grated Parmesan and black pepper.

Serves 4.

STUFFED BRIOCHES

25 g (1 oz/6 teaspoons) butter
1 clove garlic, crushed
6 spring onions, coarsely chopped
1 teaspoon pickled green peppercorns, drained
85 g (3 oz) baby button mushrooms, sliced
4 teaspoons dry vermouth
150 ml (5 fl oz/⅔ cup) thick sour cream
115 g (4 oz) cooked chicken, sliced
1 small red pepper (capsicum), deseeded, skinned and sliced
salt and cayenne pepper
1 tablespoon chopped fresh chervil
6 individual brioches, tops removed and filling scooped out

Preheat oven to 180C (350F/Gas 4). In a frying pan, melt the butter and gently sauté the garlic, onions, peppercorns and mushrooms until slightly softened. Stir in the vermouth and allow to boil, then add the thick sour cream and simmer until reduced and thickened. Stir in the chicken and pepper (capsicum) and cook for a further 5 minutes. Season with salt and cayenne pepper and stir in the chervil.

Spoon the chicken filling into the brioches, replace the tops, place on a baking sheet and cover with foil. Bake in the oven for 10 minutes. Serve warm, garnished with sprigs of chervil.

Serves 6.

CHICKEN ITALIENNE

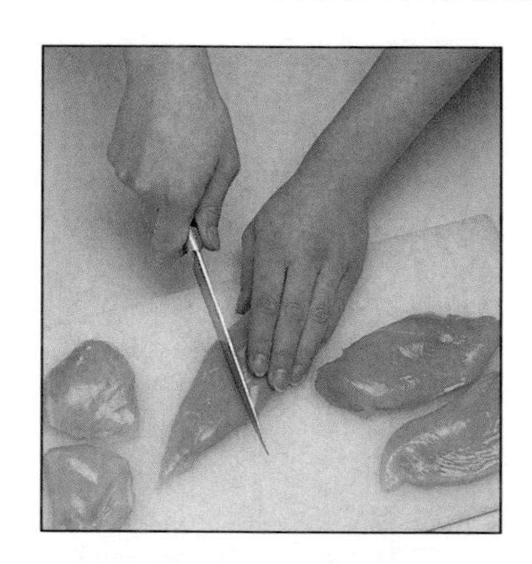

4 boned and skinned chicken breasts
8 slices Parma ham
bunch of fresh sage
175 g (6 oz) dolcelatte cheese, cut into 4 slices
freshly ground black pepper
2 tablespoon olive oil

Cut each chicken breast in half and flatten slightly by beating between 2 sheets of greaseproof paper with a rolling pin.

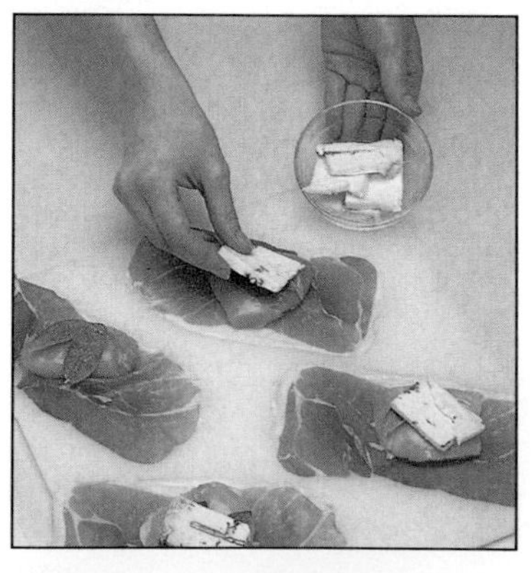

Lay the slices of Parma ham on a board. Put a piece of chicken in the middle of each slice and place 2 or 3 fresh sage leaves on the chicken and top with a slice of dolcelatte. Season with pepper. Wrap the Parma ham around the chicken to form a parcel.

Heat the oil in a frying pan, add the chicken and fry for 3-4 minutes on each side until the chicken is cooked and the cheese has melted.

Serves 4.

CHICKEN PROVENÇALE

25 g (1 oz/6 teaspoons) butter
1 tablespoon oil
6 cloves garlic, unpeeled
4 chicken joints, cut in half
115 ml (4 fl oz/½ cup) medium sherry
400 g (14 oz) can chopped tomatoes
2 tablespoons tomato purée (paste)
2 tablespoons chopped fresh herbs
salt and pepper

In a large pan, heat the butter and oil, add the garlic and the chicken, skin-sides down, and cook for 15 minutes on one side until the chicken is half cooked.

Add the sherry to the pan and boil rapidly until reduced by half. Turn the chicken pieces over and continue to boil until the sherry is reduced to a syrup.

Add the tomatoes and tomato purée (paste) and continue cooking for a further 15 minutes until the chicken is tender and the sauce has reduced to a glaze. Add the chopped herbs and season with a little salt and pepper. Serve with saffron rice and French beans.

Serves 4.

CHICKEN FRICASSÉE

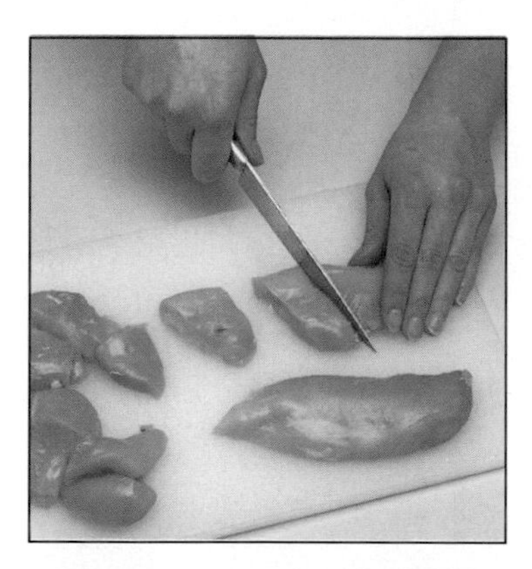

4 boned and skinned chicken breasts
15 g (½ oz/3 teaspoons) butter
½ tablespoon oil
12 small shallots, halved
175 g (6 oz) shiitake mushrooms, sliced
1 tablespoon plain flour
55 ml (2 fl oz/¼ cup) dry white wine
150 ml (5 fl oz/⅔ cup) chicken stock
150 ml (5 fl oz/⅔ cup) double (thick) cream
1 tablespoon chopped fresh chervil or parsley
juice of ½ lemon
salt and pepper

Cut each chicken breast into 4 pieces. In a pan, heat the butter and oil, add the chicken and fry over a high heat until golden.

Remove from the pan and put to one side. Add the shallots to the pan and fry for 3-4 minutes until starting to turn golden. Add the mushrooms and cook for a further 2 minutes. Sprinkle over the flour and cook for 1 minute. Gradually add the white wine and chicken stock. Bring to the boil, stirring, and cook for 2 minutes until the sauce thickens slightly.

Return the chicken and any juices to the pan. Add the cream and simmer for 10-12 minutes until the chicken is tender. Add the chervil or parsley, lemon juice and salt and pepper. Serve hot.

Serves 4.

- SPINACH & RICOTTA CHICKEN -

1 shallot, chopped
2 tablespoons olive oil
1 teaspoon fennel seeds
55 g (2 oz) ricotta cheese
25 g (1 oz) pine nuts, toasted and chopped
115 g (4 oz) finely chopped, cooked spinach
4 chicken breasts
salt and pepper
8 rashers bacon, rinds removed
1 clove garlic, crushed
400 g (14 oz) can chopped tomatoes
2 teaspoons tomato purée (paste)
2 teaspoons sugar
2 tablespoons chopped fresh basil

In a small pan, gently fry the shallot in 1 tablespoon oil until transparent. Add the fennel seeds and cook for 30 seconds. Remove from the heat. Mix the shallot and fennel seeds with the ricotta and pine nuts. Drain the spinach well and add to the mixture; reserve. Lay the chicken breasts on a board and slice each one through the centre leaving one edge uncut so that each breast can be opened like a book. Season with salt and pepper. Spread 2 tablespoons of the spinach mixture over each breast, then roll up.

Wrap 2 rashers of bacon around each chicken breast and secure with cocktail sticks. Place in a small greased ovenproof dish and cook for 15-20 minutes. Grill for 2-3 minutes to crisp the bacon. Meanwhile, add remaining oil to a pan and cook the garlic for 30 seconds. Add the tomatoes, tomato purée (paste), sugar, and salt and pepper and simmer for 15 minutes until thicker. Adjust the seasoning and add the basil. Spoon over the chicken.

Serves 4.

TARRAGON CHICKEN

25 g (1 oz/6 teaspoons) butter
1 tablespoon oil
4 large, corn-fed chicken breasts, skinned
2 large leeks
2 tablespoons tarragon vinegar
150 ml (5 fl oz/⅔ cup) dry white wine
225 ml (8 fl oz/1 cup) chicken stock
1 large carrot, peeled
150 ml (5 fl oz/⅔ cup) crème fraîche
1 teaspoon cornflour
1 teaspoon Dijon and tarragon mustard
2 teaspoons chopped fresh tarragon
salt and pepper
tarragon sprigs, to garnish

In a frying pan, heat the butter and oil and fry the chicken until golden on both sides, remove from the pan and allow to drain on absorbent kitchen paper. Coarsely chop one leek and fry gently until slightly softened, add the vinegar and boil rapidly until the quantity is reduced by half. Pour in the wine and stock and return the chicken to the pan, then cover and simmer for 25 minutes. Cut the remaining leek and the carrot into matchstick strips and cook for 4-5 minutes in separate pans of boiling, salted water; drain and refresh under cold water, then drain again.

Remove the chicken from the pan and arrange on a warmed serving dish. Strain the cooking liquor into a clean pan and bring to the boil. In a bowl, whisk together the crème fraîche, cornflour, mustard and 2 tablespoons of the pan juices. Return the mixture to the pan and add the carrots, leeks and tarragon. Heat gently until the sauce thickens and season to taste. Spoon over the chicken breasts and garnish with sprigs of tarragon.

Serves 4.

CHICKEN WITH YOGURT

150 ml (5 fl oz/⅔ cup) dry white wine
2 teaspoons English mustard
3 tablespoons chopped fresh tarragon
4 skinned and boned chicken breasts, cut into strips
1 tablespoon oil
1 tablespoon cornflour
3 tablespoons brandy
150 ml (5 fl oz/⅔ cup) Greek yogurt
salt and pepper

In a bowl, mix the white wine with the mustard and tarragon. Add the chicken, mix well, cover and refrigerate for 3-4 hours. Drain and reserve the marinade.

Heat the oil in a pan and cook the chicken quickly without browning. Mix the cornflour to a paste with a little water and add to the pan with the brandy and the reserved marinade.

Cook over a medium heat for 12-15 minutes until the chicken is cooked through. Add the yogurt, heat through and season with a little salt and pepper. Serve hot.

Serves 4.

MARSALA LIVERS

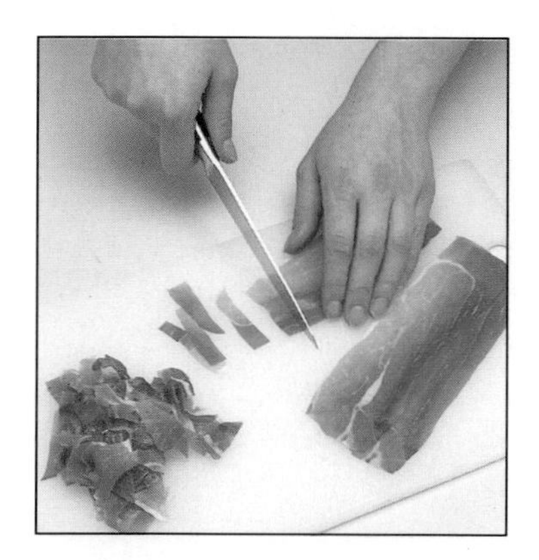

450 g (1 lb) chicken livers, cores removed
1 tablespoon well-seasoned plain flour
25 g (1 oz/6 teaspoons) butter
2 teaspoons olive oil
1 red onion, thinly sliced
115 g (4 oz) button mushrooms, sliced
55 g (2 oz) Parma ham, cut into thin slices
2 teaspoons fresh thyme leaves, plus sprigs to garnish
85 ml (3 fl oz/⅓ cup) Marsala
225 ml (8 fl oz/1 cup) chicken stock
1-2 teaspoons Worcestershire sauce
2 teaspoons tomato purée (paste)
salt and pepper
tagliatelle, to serve
150 ml (5 fl oz/⅔ cup) thick sour cream
cayenne pepper

Toss the chicken livers in the flour. In a pan, heat the butter and oil and gently fry the onion until softened. Remove from the pan and set aside. Increase the heat and fry the floured livers until well browned, then reduce the heat, return the onions to the pan and add any remaining flour, the mushrooms, Parma ham and thyme and stir well.

Pour in the Marsala and stock and bring to the boil, stirring continuously. Stir in the Worcestershire sauce and tomato purée (paste) and season to taste. Cook the tagliatelle, drain and arrange on a warmed serving plate, top with the livers and spoon over the thick sour cream. Sprinkle with a little cayenne pepper and garnish with sprigs of thyme.

Serves 4.

CHICKEN WITH CRAB

4 skinned and boned chicken breasts
175 g (6 oz) white and brown crabmeat
2 spring onions, finely chopped
1 teaspoon tomato purée (paste)
salt and pepper
15 g (½ oz/3 teaspoons) butter
1 shallot, finely chopped
4 tablespoons brandy
1 tablespoon plain flour
2 tablespoons dry white wine
115 ml (4 fl oz/½ cup) chicken stock
175 g (6 oz) cooked peeled prawns
4 tablespoons crème fraîche
1-2 tablespoons lemon juice
1 tablespoon chopped fresh dill

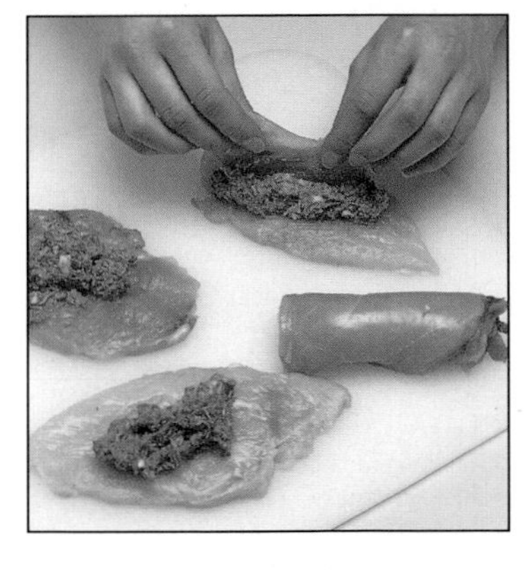

Preheat oven to 200C (400F/Gas 6). Lay the chicken breasts between 2 sheets of greaseproof paper and beat out with a rolling pin to about 0.5 cm (¼ in) thick. Mix the crabmeat with the spring onions and tomato purée (paste) and seasoning. Place 2-3 tablespoons of the crab mixture along the length of each breast and roll up to enclose the filling. Cut squares of foil larger than each chicken breast. Brush with oil and roll tightly around each breast, twisting the ends to seal. Place in an ovenproof dish and bake for 12-15 minutes until cooked.

Melt the butter in a small pan and fry the shallot for 2 minutes. Add the brandy and boil rapidly to reduce the liquid by half. Stir in the flour, then gradually add the wine and stock and bring to the boil, stirring until the sauce has thickened. Add the prawns and crème fraîche and simmer for 2 minutes. Add the lemon juice, dill and seasoning. Remove the chicken from the foil, adding any juices to the sauce. Slice the chicken breasts, fan out and spoon over the sauce.

Serves 4.

INDEX